EMPOWERED

DEVELOPING STRONG WOMEN
FOR KINGDOM SERVICE

ANDREA SCHWARTZ

CHALCEDON / ROSS HOUSE BOOKS
VALLECITO, CALIFORNIA

With appreciation to my "adopted mom,"

Dorothy Ross Rushdoony,

who encouraged me to be a Titus 2 older woman.

Contents

I

Restoring Women to Full Citizenship in the Kingdom of God

There is a perspective within Christian circles that espouses the idea that men should never learn from women or seriously consider what they say. There is an unspoken rule that, when it comes to theology, women should take a backseat and let men do the heavy lifting. The underlying assumption is that women should only concern themselves with meal preparation, maintaining the home, and caring for children. This is a hard perspective to justify, considering the words of Jesus in Luke 10:38–42:

> Now as they went on their way, Jesus entered a village. And a woman named Martha welcomed him into her house. And she had a sister called Mary, who sat at the Lord's feet and listened to his teaching. But Martha was distracted with much serving. And she went up to him and said, "Lord, do you not care that my sister has left me to serve alone? Tell her then to help me." But the Lord answered her, "Martha, Martha, you are anxious and troubled about many things, but *one thing is necessary. Mary has chosen the good portion, which will not be taken away from her.*"

It is unfortunate that many women are denied the "good portion" when it comes to conferences or other learning venues because they are too concerned with serving food, or taking care of little ones.

Why don't we make it a priority that wives, mothers, and daughters receive the same opportunity to grow in their faith as their male counterparts?

Failing to ensure that women receive equal opportunity to learn the law-word of God and its practical applications in their lives makes them easier targets for those who would prey upon them physically, emotionally, and sexually. Many have contributed worthwhile perspectives from many different angles on the subject of abuse,[1] and this essay will not attempt to cover that ground. The purpose is to offer a preventative perspective that will bolster girls and women to halt potentially detrimental situations before they become harmful and damaging.

It is not always true that the enemy of my enemy is my friend. I suggest that by riding the pendulum against feminism too far to the right, many have advocated a *de facto* underclass status for women, denying them the fullest opportunity to become well-versed in the law-word of God and in the expression of their gifts. At times, it goes so far as to assert that women should never be in a position to instruct men. I, for one, have received criticism for addressing attendees at a conference on Biblical law. The reason for criticism: I am a woman and should not be teaching men. No complaint was levelled against what I said or how I said it, merely that my gender disqualified me.

I was addressing the implications of Proverbs 31, and by no means exercising spiritual authority over men. These criticisms were not made directly to me face-to-face, and surprisingly came from both men and women. I wish I had been confronted personally. I would have informed my critics that I had proceeded with the approval of my husband and the other speakers (all male) at the conference. They saw no problem with my filling in for a speaker who was unable to fulfill his commitment. After all, this was not a church service, and I was not preaching.[2]

Let me explain why the criticisms illustrate faulty presuppositions.

1. See Martin Selbrede, "Liberty from Abuse," at www.chalcedon.edu.
2. This talk, "The Role of Mothers in Building a Kingdom-Driven Family," is included as Chapter 11 of this book.

1. The mother is the primary caregiver and instructor for an infant from the outset of life. Thus, from the get-go, females (mothers) are teaching their sons. This is a civilizing enterprise that, when done Biblically, increases the likelihood that boys will eventually take their place as godly husbands and fathers.

2. While the Scripture tells older women to teach younger women to teach what is good, and train young women to love their husbands and children, to be self-controlled, pure, working at home, kind, and submissive to their own husbands (Titus 2), this does not preclude that their instruction may also be of benefit to men.

3. While it is the norm in the Bible that men are the leaders and providers for families, there are noteworthy examples of women stepping up in the absence of men, when men were deceased, derelict and/or wicked in their duties, or when special opportunities arose.[3]

In many of the mentoring relationships I enjoy with women, husbands and fathers have often thanked me for the perspective I bring and the gain they, as men, have had from what I teach. I always encourage women to share the fruits of our sessions with their spouse or parent to maintain the structure, priority, and integrity of the family. What should qualify me or disqualify me from this role is not my gender, but my knowledge, understanding, and application of the law-word of God.[4]

When I begin a study of Biblical law with an individual woman or a group, my initial session establishes that my goal is *not* that they end up thinking exactly as I do. I emphasize that the Word of God must reign supreme, and that they are responsible to be faithful in their learning, application, and transmission to others. By understanding how to apply the law-word of God, a woman is more

---

3. Deborah, Jael, Abigail, and Esther come to mind as examples. Clearly in the case of Esther, she acted in a role no man would have been able to fill in her special circumstance.

4. Some might cite 1 Cor. 14:34 in defense of my critics. While Paul's admonition for women to keep silence in the churches, does not apply to my talk at the conference nor women speaking anywhere else, it is important to understand the context of his remarks and their application for today. This is a discussion worthy of more than an endnote. My response to the passage cited is to understand it in terms of 1 Cor. 11:5, reconciling Paul's meaning by considering both.

protected from anyone who would attempt to dominate or oppress her. No one has the right to ask people to conform to his or her will and ideas. However, we do have the responsibility to summon people to conform to God's Word and calling.

Our Kingdom Calling

Any discussion about the roles of men and women in furthering the Kingdom of God must begin in the area of calling. Unfortunately, modern thinking identifies as calling what one does for pay or by way of a career or profession. This is especially myopic in that it confuses making a living with the purpose for living. The Westminster Catechism tells us that we all have a duty to glorify God by loving Him and keeping His commandments.[5] Thus, to find one's calling is to embrace fully all the lawful ways in which a person, using his gifts, talents, and inclinations, serves the Kingdom of God.

There are certain callings that are ours at birth. One is either a son or daughter, and possibly a brother or sister from the outset. There are those besides our parents with whom we have a relationship because of our birth. This includes grandparents, aunts, uncles, and cousins. We can add husband, wife, and in-laws at the point of marriage, along with colleagues, friends, and acquaintances. All these relationships are callings and with varying rules of engagement. Nevertheless, all relationships are to be governed by the law-word of God, carrying with them certain unchangeable requirements. So in the truest sense, people do not need to find their calling; they need to embrace their most fundamental calling of fearing God and keeping His commandments (Eccles. 12:13).

Prior to the Reformation, the perspective was that *calling* was limited to the ecclesiastical realm, making the clergy the only people with holy vocations. R. J. Rushdoony observes,

> The anointing of persons and things set them apart for God's use. The term used by the Reformers for this in the lives of all of us is *vocation*.

---

5. Westminster Shorter Catechism, questions 1–3.

While serving God in any and every line of work has penalties in a fallen world, it also means that God's vocation for us is also our "oil of gladness." It is our way of holiness.[6]

Rushdoony notes that we must look to God's Word and the Holy Spirit as the only reliable guides when it comes to identifying and living out our callings.

> The enemies of Christianity have too often determined the agenda for discussion, and the subject of predestination has been restricted to election to salvation or reprobation, and to free will versus predestination... [P]redestination also has to do with our abilities... They are God-ordained and an aspect of our calling, so that God is more involved in our skills than we are.[7]

> The Holy Spirit thus has a more general as well as a more specific place in our lives and world than is generally recognized. The doctrine of vocation or calling must be seen as essentially related to the Holy Spirit. We are therefore not alone; whatever our gifts or vocation, however great or small, we are the instruments of the Holy Spirit. To limit the Spirit's manifestations in our lives to dramatic or ecstatic experiences is to limit severely our relationship to Him. He is very much present in all our daily tasks, and we have the duty to recognize His presence and power.[8]

Too often, Christian parents, in a human attempt to right the wrongs of a rebellious culture, limit the Holy Spirit by determining for their children (specifically daughters) what callings are suitable for them. In many cases, these limitations have more to do with parents' personal preference rather than teaching their children how to hear God's particular call to on their lives.

Helping Children Discover Their Particular Calling

I used to tell my children that adulthood would mean that they would be the responsible parties when it came to obedience and

---

6. R. J. Rushdoony, *Exodus* (Vallecito, CA: Ross House Books, 2004), 454.
7. ibid., 457–458.
8. ibid., 459.

disobedience. While they were young, it was our job as parents to act as stewards for them, but that was temporary. Because my children were familiar with the concept of leaving messages on a phone answering machine (before the days of voicemail), I told them that God was not going to leave a message for them on my machine; they would have to learn how to retrieve their own messages.

This developed into a writing assignment that I not only used with my three children, but also with others I tutored privately or in co-op settings. Here is the assigned essay:

> Usually students are required to write essays about what they want to be when they grow up. Younger students often have grandiose ideas of careers without any real understanding of what their choice entails. Older students may have some idea, but usually have not thought through the particulars, such as prerequisites or minimum requirements. To help in this pursuit, follow steps 1, 2, and 3 and then write a cohesive essay entitled, "What God Is Calling Me to Do."
>
> 1) Determine your particular (as opposed to general) calling under God. You may already have some idea of what God is calling you to do. You may need to begin this assignment in prayer. If nothing apparent comes to mind, take stock of the interests and talents God has given you to help identify your particular calling.
>
> 2) Research the calling or profession by finding articles, books, or journals that describe what is involved.
>
> 3) Interview (informally) someone who is actively living out such a calling. Questions to that person should include: necessary prerequisites, pitfalls to watch out for, costs involved, personal benefits, potential drawbacks, difficulty in advancement, and any recommendations for reading, training, or overall preparation.

After completing the assignment, many students determined the need to revisit their sense of their particular calling. This did not mean the assignment was a failure. It had provided an opportunity to learn how to hear from God. This assignment encourages a deliberate approach to Kingdom service, and makes it possible to instill a sense of responsibility in young people. I was always careful to take their responses at face value, not belittling choices they made. It was not my job to live their lives for them. I was eager for them to explore, without preconceived notions, what God might have in store for them.

Preparation for a Godly Calling

[B]ecause blessings are in terms of God's providential government and care, we can, by faithfully living in terms of God's grace and law-word, bless God by serving Him and being His ministers in our respective vocations. Psalm 103 calls for us to bless God with all our being in gratitude and joy. The offertory hymn, "We Give Thee but Thine Own," sums up the essence of man blessing God by his grateful spirit and acts.[9]

As the Christian church has abandoned the idea that our faith is a faith for all of life, we have had generations of Christians adapting to the world's agenda when it comes to using the gifts and abilities God has given us. In our day, rare are institutions of higher learning that prepare students to be self-consciously Christian in all areas of life and thought. As a result, our solutions and projects are often governed by a secular worldview instead of a Biblical worldview. As a result, very few adults can succinctly state how their respective vocations bless God with their entire being in gratitude and joy.

Rushdoony points out,

The Reformation doctrines of justification by faith, the priesthood of all believers, and the Christian calling and vocation made possible the potential coincidence of the kingdom and the world as an historical objective, not, of course, to be fully realized in this life, but to be approximated and the proper goal of historical activity. Thus the Reformation was liberation and the promise of life, but a promise thus far unrealized. Why this failure? Even as Roman Catholicism has historically absorbed local deities at times as saints, and absorbed local goddesses into the image of the Madonna, so Protestantism has followed a similar policy with regard to secularism. It has tried to make the world over into the kingdom by baptizing paganism and secularism, by sprinkling a few drops of approval and benediction over the heads of alien

---

9. ibid., 540.

philosophies and presuppositions. It has operated on the principle of common ground rather than reconquered ground. It has borrowed its doctrines of education from the world, its political theory from the state, its concept of the law from pharisaism, secularism, and Thomism. In the early 1930s, some New Deal economists asserted that the road to prosperity and wealth was through unlimited spending and debt. Similar reasoning seems to prevail in many Christian circles: the more we allow the world to prevail in the church, the stronger the church! The more we throw away our Christian presuppositions, the more strong our Christian strength and appeal, ostensibly! The gospel, apparently, is not big enough or wide enough to meet the world in its own strength; it must borrow Saul's armor.[10]

Dislodging Stereotypes

We must proceed in all areas of life with accurate Biblical presuppositions and guard against baptizing our own preferences. We must resist the tendency to embrace the preferences of any celebrity, visionary guru who attempts to rule the lives of his audience and supporters. This means honestly unearthing any stereotypes we may have adopted in response to secular ones we have tried to avoid.

A prime stereotype in need of dislodging involves how the education of women is sometimes viewed in Christian, homeschooling families. Rather than offer young girls the opportunity to identify the gifts, talents, interests, and inclinations God has placed within them, they often are told that certain areas of life are out of bounds for them, and they must concentrate on domestic skills alone. In an effort to keep them from acting like card-carrying feminists, they are confined to a future that limits them to quite a bit less than what Proverbs 31 describes as a Kingdom woman.[11]

In an attempt to swing the pendulum back to Biblical standards for marriage and family, an over-correction has occurred which has

---

10. R. J. Rushdoony, *By What Standard* (Vallecito, CA: Ross House Books, [1958] 1995), 174–175.

11. See Chapter 11, "The Role of Mothers in Building a Kingdom-Driven Family," and "Proverbs 31 ~ Practical Applications for Today's Woman" at www.thekingdomdrivenfamily.com.

hampered the true expression of God's plan for the Kingdom-driven family.[12] Moreover, while it is true that the highest expression of womanhood is in the calling of wife and mother, to assert that women should not pursue proficiency and skill in additional areas of life goes beyond the dictates of Scripture. Women are not an underclass, but hold full citizenship in the Kingdom of God. St. Paul makes it very clear,

> There is neither Jew nor Greek, there is neither slave nor free, there is no male and female, for you are all one in Christ Jesus. (Gal. 3:28)

This oneness in Christ includes a woman pursuing those things that God lays on her heart, with the cooperation and blessing of the men in authority over her (father or husband). Determining that women cannot bring insight and understanding in group Bible studies, or that they should be denied the opportunity to study subjects in which they demonstrate competence and ability, hamstrings 50 percent of the population. To what end? Do we really wish to assert subservience rather than godly submission? Keeping another down does not make you stronger.

If we truly wish to raise up a generation that can advance God's Kingdom and deal with the serious issues we face in our time, we should not eliminate the potent and vibrant force that godly women can be. Ensuring their access to all opportunities to learn Biblical law should remain a top priority. Not only will it protect them from those who would seek to take advantage of them; it also will make them more competent in fulfilling the Great Commission.

---

12. See www.leslievernick.com/does-my-husband-always-have-the-final-say

2

It Is Not Good for Man to Be Alone[1]

Once, I was joking with my husband about an instance where I had followed through on something he'd forgotten to do. I commented, "Honey, God knew you'd need me. That's why I'm your wife." He laughed and I laughed. Then, I got to thinking about what I had just said and realized that, not only was it true, but I hadn't stated it completely. God did not merely know my husband would need me, He fashioned *me* and foreordained *me* to be my husband's helpmeet.

This may sound trite and obvious, but the more I thought about it, the more I realized that during those very times when I am upset with things my husband "is" or "isn't," my complaint really isn't with him, but with God. You see, part and parcel of who I am and what talents I possess has everything to do with the reality that I was fashioned to *help* my husband — my *specific* husband. What's more, in stating that it isn't good for man to be alone, God was outlining for me, and wives in general, the high calling that we've been given. In a very real sense, we were designed to fill the holes and smooth over the rough spots of the husbands God gave us.

I know some might fear that this will become an excuse for husbands to take their wives for granted or to reduce them to status of slave or servant. Steve Schlissel in his excellent sermon, "Husbands,

---

1. This essay first appeared in Chalcedon Foundation's *Faith for All of Life* magazine in the late 1990s.

Love Your Wives" (available from Messiah's Congregation), gives a wonderful description of the common traps married couples can fall into. I used to make it a point to give it as a wedding gift with a recommendation that the couples listen to it one year after they're married and once every year after that. In more than one case, husbands who have listened to the recording have come to their wives and apologized and asked for forgiveness for taking them for granted and abusing their position as husband.

I am not unaware of tendencies in some Christian circles to belittle women. In an effort to ensure that women don't assume roles in church government not properly theirs, some men assume they don't have any place in discussion or decisions. It's as though their wives' thoughts and opinions don't matter — they are merely extensions of their husbands. Women in this position will find their comfort in fulfilling their God-ordained role in realizing they were fashioned to help their particular man, whether or not they are appreciated at the moment.

Marriage is a perfect institution comprised of imperfect people. Failure to put our whole effort into glorifying God through our marriages leaves us open for most of the ills our society inflicts. Marriage and the family are the basis of society; if we want to build a culture, we must start with ourselves. Both wives and husbands need regularly to evaluate their faithfulness to the high calling given them by God.

3

Power On Her Head: The Home Field Advantage

> Most of what passes for "restoring male leadership in the church" these days is in fact suppressing female initiative and decreasing areas of legitimate action and involvement by women. It's not difficult to predict that this won't lead to more men leaders and more obedient wives but to more complacent and tyrannical men and more frustrated wives. You can't make a leader out of a man by telling his wife what she shouldn't do.[1]

Throughout history, philosophical ideas have had negative effects on family life. The Enlightenment, by demeaning woman's role, set the stage for the reactionary feminist movement, and the recent so-called patriarchy movement appears to be a hyper-reaction to feminism. Each movement skewed, exaggerated, undermined, and often ignored the Biblical perspective on the woman's role as wife and mother. In fact, what is taught from the pulpit and in Bible studies contributes to the frustration women experience in our day. There needs to be a lot of work to recover a clear understanding on marriage and the role of marriage in reclaiming the culture.

Proverbs 31 talks about a wife looking well to the ways of her household. Thus, women are the managers of their homes. Some take exception to this assertion because they consider it a usurpation

---

1. Bojidar Marinov, Facebook post November 10, 2014.

of the role of husbands as head of the household. However, the Scripture says that the man is the head of the wife (Eph. 5:23); it does not instruct him to be the manager of the household. The real usurpation actually occurs when the wife is robbed of her area of dominion, thereby disregarding her co-vicegerency alongside her husband within her sphere — the home. If a woman is nothing more than her husband's stand-in, rather than his full partner in all matters, not only is the dominion mandate lessened in the home, but the surrounding culture is affected, as well.

Business enterprises have owners, general managers, and department managers. Whether it is a restaurant, a hospital, a car dealership, or a sports team, there is a chain of authority that is defined, along with job descriptions outlining roles and responsibilities. When run well, those higher up in the chain of command allow those who are in subordinate positions to do their jobs without bypassing them or interfering.

Because we have lost the high view of women outlined in Scripture, we are left with women being much more akin to slaves than full partners with their husbands. This negates the statement by God in Genesis that it is not good that the man should be alone. As I argued in an earlier essay, "Loyal Opposition,"[2] the woman's role is to be a useful reflection of her husband, so that she can serve in a corrective capacity in the case of an intentional or inadvertent transgression by him of God's law.

A Biblical Example

In 1 Samuel we have the account of Abigail assuming authority and setting policy when her husband acted recklessly and insulted David (1 Sam. 25). Rather than sit back and allow her entire family and community to reap the consequences of Nabal's foolishness, she executed her authority by directing considerable amount of the family wealth and possessions to appease David's anger. In the process,

---

2. See Andrea Schwartz, *A House for God: Building a Kingdom-Driven Family* (Vallecito, CA: Chalcedon/Ross House Books, 2014), 66–76.

her actions not only saved those she cared for, but convicted David that the move he was about to make would have been wrong. Abigail is a good illustration of a wife's power — a power that is recognized by God and respected by men.

For certain, not all Christian men are of Nabal's poor character. But how often do they fail to see the big picture or consult their wives when important decisions that will affect more than just themselves arise? Part of the gift of a wife to a husband (Prov. 18:22) is an extra set of loyal eyes to help him as he works to advance the culture for Christ and His Kingdom.

Foundation of the Family Is the Foundation of the Culture

When two people contemplate marriage they should spend time ensuring that their worldviews and application of God's law-word are in harmony with each other. This will help avoid problems of priority and practice in the marriage. The man needs to ask himself if the woman he is considering shares his vision for his calling of dominion. He should desire a woman who is versed in Biblical law and who has experience applying it to all aspects of life, and who is willing to be a full-partner in whatever he is involved in. The woman needs to determine if the man she is considering loves God enough to stand on His Word faithfully and is looking for a wife who does likewise. She needs to observe whether or not a prospective spouse is already exercising dominion in his calling, willing to stand for God's truth and not compromising just to get ahead. She needs to see that the person whose covering she will be under respects her and welcomes her full participation in all aspects of the marriage.[3]

This is contrary to the modern, humanistic view that romantic love and social status should constitute the basis for marriage. Rushdoony points out,

Love, in [the] Biblical sense means, moreover, that the basis of the

---

3. The Biblical dowry served to demonstrate the earnestness of the man in the proposal of marriage. Although too extensive a discussion for the purpose of this essay, see R. J. Rushdoony, the *Institutes of Biblical Law*, vol. 1, 176ff., 363ff., 417.

marriage and of the new family is not personal but Christian. In romantic love, the family is started when romantic feeling draws a man and woman together, and it ends with the death of those feelings. Marriage is thus made a purely personal affair. But the family is a God-given institution and it is the basic social institution. No decision concerning the family therefore can be purely personal. At all times, the family is under God's law, and its beginning and ending must be in terms of obedience to God's law.[4]

This perspective can be expanded to include the wife having a stake and a say in all aspects of the decisions of the family. Could it be that our modern aberration of this fact is a significant reason that we don't see more evidence of dominion-taking on the part of Christian men? Could their focus be too inwardly directed toward the day-to-day affairs of their families, abandoning their roles in the public square? In the process of usurping the position of the wife in many matters, husbands abandon their primary focus of working in their cultural dominion calling.

Bojidar Marinov has pointed out that

A brief theological analysis of the covenantal position of the wife in the family is necessary...A wife is not a simple addendum to the family, as she was in the pagan, patriarchal times. She is one with her husband, in everything, and especially in the management of his property. In fact, she is so united to him that she is a *co-owner* of his property, and *by default*—not by delegation, as some incorrectly claim—she holds sovereign rights over his property, mitigated only by his right to veto her decisions (Num. 30). The veto, however, has certain limitations on the husband (not on the wife), and failure to confirm or to annul her actions leads to automatic confirmation, that is, a decision of favor of the wife's actions. Outside of that veto, the wife's decisions are as good as the husband's decisions, when management of the home is concerned.[5]

In many Christian circles, there are women who are certain that

4. R. J. Rushdoony, *Law & Liberty* (Vallecito, CA: Ross House Books, [1984] 2009), 107.

5. Bojidar Marinov, "Eschatology and the Covenantal Status of the Church" in *Faith for All of Life*, May/June 2013.

they cannot make any important decisions on their own. Often this is how they have been instructed. When the power of the wife is minimized, trampled upon, or nonexistent, her status is much more akin to a concubine than wife, in that she is not viewed as a full partner in the marriage, but merely as the baby maker, child care provider, maid, cook, etc.

Marinov continues,

> A concubine in the Old Testament was a wife who was given in marriage without a dowry, that is, without her own economic or financial stake in the new family. She had no inheritance, and her children had no inheritance in the family. For all covenantal purposes, a concubine was a servant. And indeed, while as a legal wife she was entitled to food, clothes, and "duty of marriage" (Exod. 21:7–11), she didn't have the same authority in her husband's household as the wife. The story of Sarah and Hagar very plainly shows this truth. She couldn't rule the house as a wife, unless her husband delegated that task to her. This, of course, would put her in a position of being a servant to the true wife who could rule the house. The concubine was a servant to the wife, as Hagar was to Sarah.[6]

The Bible gives the woman of the house the status of house manager in that she is commanded to look well to the ways of her household. This position is one of authority and decision making and, while being under the authority of her husband, she has a domain that even he needs to respect and not undermine.

> The virtuous wife in Proverbs 31 is described as one who freely administers the property of the family while her husband is away. The lack of direct involvement by the husband there doesn't necessarily mean that he shouldn't get involved; but it does reveal the covenantal principle that the wife is fully empowered to make decisions without asking her husband for permission. Paul admonishes the young women to get married and "rule a house," (1 Tim. 5:14; the word in Greek is literally a "house despot").[7]

R. J. Rushdoony explains, in his comments on Proverbs 31,

---

6. ibid.
7. ibid.

The Biblical doctrine shows us the wife as the competent manager who is able to take over all business affairs if needed, so that her husband can assume public office as a civil magistrate; in the words of Prov. 31:23, he can "sit in the gates," that is, preside as a ruler or judge.[8]

Far from the Enlightenment view of a woman as being ornamental or an add-on to the family, the Biblical doctrine of women puts forth the image of one who rules alongside her husband in household, property, and business enterprises. With her focus being the care of the family, she enables her husband to make a difference in the surrounding culture, bringing to bear God's law-word.

In addition to having an overly romantic view of marriage, few today recognize the importance of Biblical marriage as central to reconstructing the culture. Is it any wonder that the church has a difficult time in standing up to arguments in favor of same-sex marriage when it fails to teach why and how the wife is integral to the dominion mandate? Her role is not a purely personal one when it comes to her husband and her main emphasis is not on her purity or spirituality. As Marinov states,

> True, a wife is supposed to keep herself pure. But her main concern after the marriage is not purity itself. Her main concern is *rulership and management*. The Proverbs 31 woman is not described in terms of her successful resistance to temptations, or her mystical spirituality, or her participation in prayer events or Bible groups. She is described as a manager of a household.
>
> A legal wife . . . owns all things together with her Husband; and she has full authority over them *by default*, by the very nature of her covenantal and redeemed position. She is expected to take charge as the virtuous wife of Proverbs 31. Her Husband is in the gates, sitting as a Judge of the world. She is over His property, bringing all things to obey the household rules, that is, the Law of God.[9]

---

8. R. J. Rushdoony, *Institutes of Biblical Law*, vol. 1 (Phillipsburg, NJ: The Presbyterian & Reformed Publishing Company, 1973), 352.
9. Marinov, ibid.

A Personal Example

My husband has worked in sales for most of our married life, and has commented to me on a number of occasions how integral my support and counsel have been to him in his professional life. He has told me that my ability and willingness to share aspects of his dominion calling on his job has made it possible for him to be faithful to God's Word when challenged by customers, coworkers, or superiors. Because he knows I support building the Kingdom of God, he feels free to be bold in sharing his faith and Biblical worldview.

In the process, I have been the person who handles the family finances and has kept us out of debt for decades. I am responsible to pay our tithes and offerings, along with making decisions regarding health, nutrition, and fellowship opportunities. It has always been a priority for me to have my husband's trust (Prov. 31:11) as I look well to the ways of our household (Prov. 31:27). And although we have had our bumps and bruises along the way, the fact that we both have a passionate desire to keep the commandments of God has allowed us to weather the storms of marriage that are part and parcel of the relationship.

A Proper View of Marriage

This perspective is not at odds with the Scriptural position of the husband as head of the wife. On the contrary, it presupposes that each will take his or her participation in their marriage's dominion calling seriously enough to focus on the Kingdom of God rather than competing with each other.

Rushdoony, as he discusses the principle of life, points out that regarding the relationship of husband and wife,

> The knowledge required of husbands in dwelling with their wives is not a knowledge of feminine psychology, but of the word of God. Here, too, the principle of life is associated with the government and authority of God and our rest therein. Most men today cannot rule in the Lord because they are unwilling themselves to submit to God's rule

and to rest in Him. They are either tyrants, ruling according to their word, or they are hen-pecked and ruled by their wives. No man has any authority in and of himself over any woman, or anything. All authority is from God and must be exercised according to His word. Too many men assume it is godly to rule a woman for their convenience. They forget that the Biblical standard of authority is ruling to serve (Matt. 20:28; Luke 22:26; John 13:1–17, etc.). Too many husbands are tyrants, not godly heads of households. Clearly, Ephesians 5:21–23 requires that the husband rule with the same self-sacrificing spirit as Christ the church. He must serve the Lord, and meet his wife's needs in the Lord. If not, the grace of life is denied.

Similarly, the wife must serve her husband as he serves the Lord. To rebel against his obedience to the Lord is to rebel against God Himself and manifest a reprobate heart.

A major problem in our time is such rebellion by wives and husbands. To illustrate, a very considerable percentage of married seminarians have major problems with their wives, who refuse to agree to their calling and show it by rejecting the conditions of their husband's calling. They refuse to go to the mission field, or to a city church, or a country church, or away from family and friends. In the name and under the cover of objecting to the terms of their husband's calling, they are denying God in a disguised but real warfare. It is their goal to break their husband and laugh at their victory over God. A reprobate heart produces reprobate courses of action...

All such women are manifesting a reprobate nature, and they can never be dealt with until this is recognized. Men who submit to such wives become castaways, useless to God because they are unfaithful to Him. Peter is clear-cut: the prayers of all such couples are not heard by God, and they are denied the grace of life. God's principle of life rests on His authority and government, and our rest therein. Parents are required to rule according to God's law and themselves to be under Him and His law. Husband and wife, in their relationship one to another, must likewise be in submission to the Lord, resting in Him, content and giving thanks, or else they will fall prey to a "root of bitterness" (Heb. 12:15) which will destroy them.[10]

---

10. R. J. Rushdoony, *Institutes of Biblical Law*, vol. 2, *Law & Society* (Vallecito, CA: Ross House Books, 1982), 505–506.

God's design for the family is specifically to further the Kingdom of God. Thus the emphasis of both husband and wife needs to be in enhancing each other's ability to serve God in their appointed roles and dominion spheres. 1 Corinthians 11:9–10 speaks of the woman being created for the man, in that God proclaimed in Genesis that is was not good for man to be alone. Furthermore, it is said that she should have a symbol of power on her head. The question remains, power for what purpose? Surely it is for more than cooking and cleaning and raising her children, for Proverbs 31 gives a much more expanded explanation of what a worthy woman is to concern herself with.

When men and women realize that God wants much more than what we are currently giving Him, and change the basis upon which we operate, we may yet see the transformation of the culture so many of us prayerfully desire.

4

So That Your Prayers Are Not Hindered

I know many godly women who have made it a priority to submit to their husbands as part of their faithful service as Christians. There are many passages in Scripture that support this concept, and yet Colossians 3:18 stands out for its clarification: "Wives, submit to your husbands, *as is fitting* in the Lord [emphasis mine]."

What does this mean? Well, it most definitely applies to the structure of the family as ordained by God. In other words, it is proper (fitting) that wives respect the role God ordained for them from the beginning: as a helper in a supportive, subordinate capacity. Yet, "fitting" also has reference to the idea that wives should submit to their husbands *in accordance* with God's law-word, rather than submitting to the whims of their spouse. This means that a woman needs to know God's law and apply it in her life.

Problems often arise when a husband and wife have differing views as to what is *in accordance* with God's law-word. Anticipating the eventual occurrence of disagreements along these lines, couples need to prepare for how they will resolve problems if/when they arise. Too often, the conclusion is reached that whatever the husband decides must always take precedence. I believe this perspective needs qualification so that God's Word is truly honored.

1 Peter 3:7 reads,

Likewise, husbands, live with your wives in an understanding way, showing honor to the woman as the weaker vessel, since they are heirs with you of the grace of life, so that your prayers may not be hindered.

When a couple has differing viewpoints as to how a particular doctrine or principle of Scripture needs to be applied, this verse is crucial to coming to a point of agreement. Here the husband is instructed not to "run over" his wife's opinion and dominate her because he is in a position to do so. The fact that she is the "weaker" vessel does not mean her perspective should be summarily ignored or overruled. The consequences of doing so actually will have profound consequences on the efficacious nature of the husband's prayers.

Couples should make it a priority to come to a point of harmony on issues such as Sabbath-keeping, tithing, and those relating to their children, etc. While orthodoxy should trump harmony, harmony remains an important aspect of married and family life. Even if a resolution takes longer to be achieved, the process of ensuring mutual respect for the other's view will make subsequent differences of opinion more easily resolved.

I cannot think of any circumstance where believers would relish having their prayers hindered. Praise God that He has provided clear instruction as to how to have our prayers heard.

5

Playing the Card

Anyone who has played Monopoly knows about the "get out of jail" card. This card allows the player to avoid the unpleasant outcome of missing a turn. In the course of the game, if a player lands on a space or draws a card sending him to jail, this card can come in handy.

Too often in life, without openly acknowledging it, we all seek to have such "cards" in reserve and pull them out when it suits us. More than once during mentoring times with wives, I hear about husbands pulling out the "submission card" on them, virtually ending all discussion. Does the Bible teach that God gives husbands such a "submission card"? If so, where do we find it? Moreover, what does it entail? Does God give women a "you are not being loving to me" card of their own to justify actions that stem from frustration when their husbands are not being loving to them?

In Ephesians 5:22–33, St. Paul lays out the basic premises to bring about harmony in marriage.

> Wives, submit to your own husbands, as to the Lord. For the husband is the head of the wife even as Christ is the head of the church, his body, and is himself its Savior. Now as the church submits to Christ, so also wives should submit in everything to their husbands.
>
> Husbands, love your wives, as Christ loved the church and gave himself up for her, that he might sanctify her, having cleansed her by the washing of water with the word, so that he might present the church to himself in splendor, without spot or wrinkle or any such thing, that she

might be holy and without blemish. In the same way husbands should love their wives as their own bodies. He who loves his wife loves himself. For no one ever hated his own flesh, but nourishes and cherishes it, just as Christ does the church, because we are members of his body. "Therefore a man shall leave his father and mother and hold fast to his wife, and the two shall become one flesh." This mystery is profound, and I am saying that it refers to Christ and the church. However, let each one of you love his wife as himself, and let the wife see that she respects her husband.

Anyone who has been married for any length of time knows that these directives are impossible to attain apart from regeneration. In other words, these are instructions to act beyond our sinful inclinations, responding to the guidance of the Holy Spirit. However, the Scripture nowhere contains a directive to husbands to enforce a wife's submission. Nor does it direct a wife to reprove or correct her husband for failing to love her as Christ loves His church. These commands to submit and to love are directed to each partner in the marriage by the Word, and are a matter of individual obedience on the part of husband and wife to the Lord.

Too often, couples use this portion of Scripture to bludgeon each other, pointing out where the other party is failing, rather than rectifying their own areas of non-compliance. This is a prime example of focusing on the speck in another's eye while living comfortably with the plank in your own (Luke 6:41–42). A spouse is not free to disregard the directive particular to him/her based on the other person's dereliction of duty. Therefore, in essence, there is no such thing as the "submission card," or the "love me card."

It is useful to examine the difference between submitting to authority and being a submissive individual. By way of analogy, if I am driving down the freeway and I see a car behind me marked as a highway patrol car with the lights on, I know that I am to pull over to the side of the road. I do this because I am submitting to the authority of the highway patrol. If I am told that I was driving too fast, and I disagree (let's say I had my cruise control on and I know I wasn't), I should not be required to say, "Yes, Officer, you are right I was speeding." That would amount to being submissive to what he/

she alleged disregarding what I know to be true. I, then, can challenge the assertion of the officer without challenging his/her authority. This distinction applies to every area of life and thought, and thus is the Biblical way to be under authority.

Imagine a marital relationship where each spouse strives to outdo the other in showing honor (Rom. 12:10), even when in the midst of a disagreement! For it is in times when the two are at odds with each other that the temptation to dishonor is greatest. What does it mean to show honor? Is it a one-way street or are both parties in a marriage called to do so? The answer lies in the creation account of the institution of marriage.

God did not give Adam his wife immediately after he was created. God allowed Adam to feel his need for a counterpart of his own apart from the animals. God declared that it was not good that Adam go through life on his own and gave him one who was compatible, yet different from him—Eve. Although they were one flesh, they remained two individual people with callings separate from each other—Adam, the husband (leader, provider, and protector) and Eve his helper (nurturer and mother of all). Neither was to determine autonomously what was good and what was bad, in terms of their marriage or in any other regard.[1] God's Word, from the beginning, was to be the necessary and only standard by which to fulfill their respective callings.

> Adam in Eden no doubt had at least one pet dog from the moment of his creation as a mature man. He was created mature into a mature creation. If all he needed was someone or something to boss and to order to come at his whistle, or his beck and call, a dog would have been sufficient. But God said, "It is not good that the man should be alone; I will make him a help meet for him" (Gen. 2:18). A helpmate is not a doormat, but a subordinate and necessary partner.[2]

---

1. This is the sin of Genesis 3:5, using our own definitions of good and evil and not God's.

2. R. J. Rushdoony, *Salvation and Godly Rule* (Vallecito, CA: Ross House Books, [1983] 2004), 495–496.

Eve was created to help Adam, but nowhere in Scripture does it say that Eve was to get her direction as to how to help her husband from her husband. I believe it is a distortion of God's created order when men take it upon themselves to assume that they are righteous in demanding that their wives submit to them unquestioningly, as if they were to be some sort of robot.[3] R. J. Rushdoony notes,

> The requirement of unquestioning obedience by any human authority is a sin and defiles the very intent of God's word. The unquestioning obedience which Scripture requires is only to God, never to kings, rulers, employers, husbands, or parents. To render unquestioning obedience is sin.
>
> Obedience thus is basic to God's plan for man, but all obedience must be to the word of God: "those things which are revealed belong unto us." "The secret things" means essentially the hidden things of the future, and the "revealed" means "the unfolded issues of the day" in terms of the law-word of God (James Moffatt). In a secondary sense, however, all that the word of God forbids to us means not only the issues of the future, but also men and the things of today. We cannot treat the world as something totally ours to use: it must be used under God. We cannot treat people as our creatures. Even in marriage, in its sexual relationship, the boundary is sharply drawn. The menstruous woman cannot be taken (Lev. 18:19, 20:18): to do so is to treat her as totally man's creature, which no man can do. The woman was also guilty, if she permitted it.[4]

Thus, the basis of a godly marriage is a commitment and covenant to God's law as the primary means to live a holy life, followed closely by a commitment and covenant to serve God's Kingdom together. Without a fidelity to God's Word as the standard, circumstances of

---

3. Those who use internet sites are well aware of CAPTCHA, a challenge-response test used in computing to determine whether the user is human. Any honest examination of Proverbs 31 demonstrates that Scripture not only demands women be godly, but they exercise their jurisdictional role in marriage as a fully capable human. The Bible does not call for a robotic partner in marriage. When such is the foundation of a marriage, a husband who demands such unquestioning obedience is guilty of stealing and coveting his wife's calling, time, and conscience.

4. ibid., 497.

disagreement and/or conflict will deteriorate into an autonomous struggle for domination.

Another passage that is often cited regarding the marital relation comes from 1 Peter 3:1–7:

> Likewise, wives, be subject to your own husbands, so that even if some do not obey the word, they may be won without a word by the conduct of their wives, when they see your respectful and pure conduct. Do not let your adorning be external — the braiding of hair and the putting on of gold jewelry, or the clothing you wear — but let your adorning be the hidden person of the heart with the imperishable beauty of a gentle and quiet spirit, which in God's sight is very precious. For this is how the holy women who hoped in God used to adorn themselves, by submitting to their own husbands, as Sarah obeyed Abraham, calling him lord. And you are her children, if you do good and do not fear anything that is frightening.
>
> Likewise, husbands, live with your wives in an understanding way, showing honor to the woman as the weaker vessel, since they are heirs with you of the grace of life, so that your prayers may not be hindered.

It is important to note the fact that the first word in each directive is "likewise." The likewise has to do with what St. Peter covers in the early part of this epistle. He is speaking to all believers in terms of the necessity to go beyond the milk of the Word and learn how to apply the law of God over every area of life and thought. He addresses rulers and subjects, masters and slaves, and every other institution. Therefore, in the truest sense, no person in any position has a "divine right" to lord it over anyone else. Rather than resort to anarchy and revolution when those in authority act this way, it is the Word of God that must direct our action and response. Rushdoony notes,

> "The secret things" of God extend to our own lives and persons. We are not our own: our todays and tomorrows are totally under the government of God, and, beyond our obedience to His law-word, we have no right to demand special knowledge, reward, or privileges. Precisely because God requires us to be obedient to Him, He at the same time sets boundaries on our authority over one another and our claims upon

one another. We have Christian liberty to the degree that we have Christian obedience.[5]

Who Should Do the Teaching?

Husbands and wives need instruction and guidance in fulfilling their duties to God in their respective callings. Although God's law-word is sufficient for such instruction, St. Paul in his letter to Titus makes it clear who should be doing the teaching: older women teach the younger ones, and older men teach the younger men (Titus 2). The assumption, of course, is that those with age and experience filter both in terms of fidelity to Scripture, not replacing doctrine with personal preference. Having gone through similar circumstances themselves, older believers can offer perspective and insight. Thus, there may well be times when a wife disagrees with how her husband is providing and protecting. She may advise, but he remains responsible for those aspects. Likewise, there may be times when a husband does not like the form or manner in which his wife performs her duty as a helpmeet, but that should not nullify the duty of the wife to help, as she understands it from Scripture. Much of this can and should be learned from those God has ordained to be the teachers.

How have we lost a heritage that included men and women working together in unity, with mutual respect and honor? Rushdoony sheds some light:

> In the European tradition, rulers were compared to God, and husbands to Christ, employers to God, and priests and pastors to Christ, without any real stress on the difference between absolute and relative authority. In the American tradition, the Puritans began by resisting authority in the name of God, and they established a tradition of godly and relative authority as against idolatrous and divine right authority. As a result, America has not had the revolutions and social upheavals so common to Europe. Too many European groups in the U.S. today are reviving this dangerous tradition, wherein rulers expect people to be unquestioningly obedient, wives to be docile cows, employees to

---

5. ibid.

bow and scrape before their employers, and church members never to question the pastor or priest in his infallible wisdom. The result is either stupid obedience or wild rebellion.

The Puritan wives were not given to servile obedience, and they provided the strong-willed helpmeets necessary to the conquest of a continent. The Puritan men held that the Kingship of Christ was the only absolute power, and they acted on that principle.

Today, as anarchy and contempt for authority are spreading everywhere, the worst possible answer is a blasphemous and idolatrous doctrine of authority. The only valid answer to either of these two crimes is godly authority.[6]

When the Kingdom of God and His righteousness are paramount, normal day-to-day conflicts can be resolved as a husband and wife self-consciously apply God's commands. Sadly, pre-marital counseling avoids the mundane, daily issues a couple will face, and fails to spend time exploring the difference between mere abstractions and actual convicting application. Since marriage is a voluntary union (unlike being born into a family), it is incumbent upon each of the parties to resolve that they know exactly what they are promising to uphold, and have demonstrated to each other the understanding of Biblical directives and a commitment to God's Word as the only and final authority.

One might think that this perspective would prevent marriages from ever taking place, setting the stage for power struggles. On the contrary, for believers contemplating marriage, the Biblical doctrine of authority establishes a bond of mutual respect for the unique roles God has ordained for the husband and for the wife. Moreover, rather than presume a "happily ever after" mentality, there would be a strong foundation laid to weather the eventual storms of life. Obedience to the commands and ordinances of God is fundamental to the Christian life. If we wish to see our culture restored based on the family as God's primary institution, we need to get this right, moving away from a pagan mentality that asserts the powers of human beings can ever be absolute.

---

6. ibid., 497–498.

The origins of this belief are in pagan antiquity and in emperor worship. They rest in the belief in the immanent deity inherent in earthly powers. This pagan concept has infiltrated and corrupted the Biblical doctrine of obedience. It must be resisted, and the people of God must be taught that it is a sin to require unquestioning obedience, and a sin to yield it. We are not God: we cannot require or expect for ourselves the absolute obedience due unto God. We are not man's creature: we cannot yield to any man the absolute and unquestioning obedience due only unto God. The church must be cleansed of the requirement of pagan obedience or it will continue under the judgment of God.[7]

---

7. ibid., 498–499.

6

Loyal Opposition

> For when for the time ye ought to be teachers, ye have need that one teach you again which be the first principles of the oracles of God; and are become such as have need of milk, and not of strong meat. (Heb. 5:12)

The author of Hebrews reproves his listeners whom he thought should have progressed beyond the "milk" of the word. In our day, many debate which aspects of the faith constitute "milk" and "meat." Some consider the doctrines of election, predestination, or matters of eschatology to be the "meat of the word." However, I submit that these are actually the "milk" of the word, because they are concepts that, if not grasped, make for a lame and disabled theology. The "meat" has much more to do with skillfully applying the law of God to the complex issues of covenantal life. Without a knowledge and understanding of God's law, it is impossible to navigate through difficult situations, including those between a husband and a wife.

If there ever was a topic that needs sound clarification and exposition, the submission of a wife to her husband certainly qualifies. Too much of the teaching from pulpits and expositors is not grounded on the law of God, and fails to take certain Biblical accounts at face value. As in every era, many of the attitudes and conclusions are a reaction to something prevalent in the culture rather than a true application of what the Scripture states. And, as Bojidar Marinov points out, many of the prevailing attitudes have more to do with margin notes and/or headings from publishers rather than the actual Biblical passages understood from a covenantal perspective.[1]

Dealing with the subject of submission is very much like walking on a minefield. It is easy to misstep and end up blown to bits. The solution is not to avoid the topic, but to approach it with fear and trembling (much as we are to work out our salvation), to better comprehend the mind of God and put His law into practice.

Ian Hodge, in a blog piece of April 27, 2013, entitled "Marriage, Submission, and the Helper Who Opposes," offers another perspective of the meaning of the word "helpmeet," sometimes also translated as "helper."

> Submission, as it is generally understood, means a person hands over his/her will to the will of another. He/She is to align his/her will with the will of another in perfect union. Thus, in the illustration of St. Paul, there is mutual submission of husbands and wives. But as he explains this in detail he describes the husband's submission as love for his wife as Christ loves his church. A wife, on the other hand, is to submit to her husband in the same way the church is to submit to Christ. (Eph. 5:21ff.)
>
> However, it is possible to read too much into these texts if they are abstracted from everything else Scripture teaches you about man-woman relationships. And the Bible starts in Genesis 2:18 with a recognition that although God created everything "good," it was not good for man to be alone. So God made him a helper. The word in the older English translations is helpmeet. But neither "helper" nor "helpmeet" capture the not-so-subtle connotation of the Hebrew, 'ezer kenegdo (עֵזֶר כְּנֶגְדּוֹ). This literally means "help against," or "the help that opposes," and has also been translated "the helpmate opposite him."
>
> You can immediately see why "helpmeet" and "helper" are really inadequate translations, neither of which capture the "opposition" contained in the word kenegdo which means against, or oppose.[2]

1. Bojidar Marinov, sermon, "Restoring Jacob's Reputation," delivered at Church of the King, McAllen, TX. See churchofthekingmcallen.org/wp-content/uploads/2012/02/20120205.mp3

2. Ian Hodge, blog, Biblical Landmarks, entry of April 27, 2013 "Marriage, Submission and the Helper Who Opposes." See http://biblicallandmarks.com/wpl/marriage-submission-and-the-helper-who-opposes/

It would be easy to dismiss Hodge's observation because it is contrary to the customary understanding that a wife's duty is to submit to her husband's wishes without complaint or disagreement. This may be in part because of the negative connotation of the word "opposition" which unfortunately is often reduced to meaning defiance or rebellion. But Webster's 1828 *Dictionary* gives ten definitions for this word:

> **opposition**, n. [L. oppositio.]
>
> 1. Situation so as to front something else; a standing over against; *as the opposition of two mountains or buildings.*
>
> 2. The act of opposing; attempt to check, restrain or defeat. *He makes opposition to the measure; the bill passed without opposition. Will any opposition be made to the suit, to the claim or demand?*
>
> 3. Obstacle. *The river meets with no opposition in its course to the ocean.*
>
> 4. Resistance; as the opposition of enemies. *Virtue will break through all opposition.*
>
> 5. Contrariety; repugnance in principle; *as the opposition of the heart to the laws of God.*
>
> 6. Contrariety of interests, measures or designs. *The two parties are in opposition to each other.*
>
> 7. Contrariety or diversity of meaning; *as one term used in opposition to another.*
>
> 8. Contradiction; inconsistency.
>
> 9. The collective body of opposers; *in England, the party in Parliament which opposed the ministry; in America, the party that opposed the existing administration.*
>
> 10. In astronomy, the situation of two heavenly bodies, when distant from each other 180 degrees.

Hodge makes the claim that part and parcel of the design of a suitable partner for Adam was someone who could serve in the capacity of nine out of ten of Webster's definitions, excepting the last one dealing with astronomy. The declaration by God that it was not good for Adam to be without a partner/helper was precisely because Adam was not complete without his counterpart.

It is wrong to reduce the idea of a woman as a counterpart merely to the physical, sexual function that Eve would serve for Adam. Her importance involves much more, as Rushdoony points out.

> The woman is called his "help meet," his mirror; and even as he mirrors God, she mirrors him. He understands his responsibility by looking to God, and he can see how he is fulfilling his responsibilities and proving his obedience in relationship to his wife as she mirrors his nature and responsibility.[3]

This is hardly a description of the wife serving as a rubber stamp to her husband's every mandate. Rather, it presupposes that as the husband's trusted advisor, she not only has the best interests of their family in mind, but of his specifically. Thus she should oppose him when she deems it necessary to honor God and keep His commandments. Hodge continues,

> Now you can also see why so many husbands get opposition from their wives. They were designed by God to oppose him. But their opposition is to be when he strays from the Word of God and begins to falter in carrying out the God-mandated activities in his life. "Have dominion," said God. "And here's your helper to oppose you every time you steer away from this."[4]

A Handful of Examples

There are three excellent examples in Scripture of wives moving in opposition to their husbands and being vindicated because of their actions. In Genesis 21:12, Abraham had listened to his wife to have a son with her maid servant. Years later Sarah recognized the seeds of conflict between Ishmael and Isaac. She told Abraham to send Hagar and her son away. Abraham was not willing to do so. Yet, God sided with Sarah,

> And God said unto Abraham, Let it not be grievous in thy sight because of the lad, and because of thy bondwoman; in all that Sarah hath said unto thee, hearken unto her voice; for in Isaac shall thy seed be called.

---

3. Elizabeth Fellersen, ed., *Toward a Christian Marriage*, R. J. Rushdoony, "The Doctrine of Marriage" (Vallecito, CA: Ross House Books, 1972), 14.
4. Hodge, blog.

In another case, Abigail (1 Sam. 25), recognizing her husband's stubbornness and wickedness, overruled her husband's refusal to supply David and his men with provision. She thereby saved her entire household. Based on some of the prevalent writings about female submission, she would be designated as a rebellious wife. Yet after God removed her foolish husband, she became a member of David's household. Clearly, God (and David) recognized her as godly and righteous.

In each of these cases, one of a God-fearing man and the other of a fool, the role of the wife is crucial to God's plan and order.

The Virtue of Rebekah's Opposition

A vivid example of this appears in Genesis 27. Rushdoony points out that this chapter of Scripture is a sad one. But it is also a very misunderstood one, placing a "bad rap" on Rebekah for deceiving her husband as she instructed Jacob to impersonate his brother so that God's blessing reserved for Jacob would not wrongly be given to her rebellious son.[5] Upon hearing that Isaac was about to overrule God by substituting Esau, Rebekah acted.

> Determined to prevent her husband from sinning by trying to replace God's choice with his, she ordered Jacob to bring in two kids. She knew how to prepare them so as to fool Isaac, so that the blessing would go to Jacob (vv. 5–10).
>
> Jacob doubted whether such a deception would succeed. Esau was a hairy man, Jacob smoother of skin (v. 11). The blind Isaac, in placing a hand on Jacob, would know the difference, and he would then curse Jacob as a deceiver (v. 12).
>
> Rebekah's answer was "Upon me be thy curse, my son: only obey my voice, and go fetch me them" (v. 13).
>
> At this point, it is important to understand what Rebekah meant when she said, "Upon me be thy curse." Curses and blessings are covenant

---

5. In the aforementioned sermon by Bojidar Marinov, he extensively exegetes this portion of Scripture with a covenantal perspective vindicating both Jacob and Rebekah from many commentators' and publishers' negative assessments.

facts, blessings for covenant faithfulness, and curses for disobedience. An oath is a personal invocation of blessings and curses for obedience or disobedience. We can only understand Rebekah and Jacob in terms of a knowledge of the meaning of blessings and curses.

Rebekah did not expect to be cursed; she sought to prevent Isaac from bringing down a curse on his own head. Loving Isaac, she wanted to prevent him from coming under God's curse. Loving Jacob, she encouraged him to be bold because he was ordained by God to be blessed. Rebekah feared God and His possible judgment on Isaac, and also on Jacob.[6]

When this account is normally exposited, it is presented with a bias that teaches that Rebekah was a devious woman who did not submit to her husband, and who did not trust God. If it is viewed from a covenantal perspective she, instead, should be viewed as a faithful wife who stood in *opposition* to her husband who was about to disobey the living God.

Rebekah's purposes included, first, preventing Isaac from bringing God's curse on himself. The fact that Isaac was now concerned about Jacob's safety is a sure indication of a change in his stance. Second, Rebekah had enabled Jacob to make a stand, not only to get a blessing already ordained by God for him, but against his ruthless brother. Third, Rebekah wanted a godly wife for Jacob. She was not aware of the religious decline of her family, but its daughters were better than local girls.

What Rebekah did was to stand unequivocally for the covenant and its integrity. She feared God's judgment on Isaac and Jacob.

To apply present day perspectives to the events of this chapter is commonplace, but for Rebekah God's covenantal promise was paramount, and she acted accordingly. It will not do to say that her favoritism to Jacob was the reason; her concern was covenantal, and God's promise concerning Jacob was no doubt basic to her partiality to Jacob.[7]

Never does the Bible indicate that a wife is at liberty to violate the covenant in order to be considered a submitted spouse. As

---

6. R. J. Rushdoony, *Genesis* (Vallecito, CA: Ross House Books, 2002), 193.
7. ibid., 194–195.

joint-heirs, husband and wife must act in unison, each bringing their commitment to God's Word as the starting point to any discussion or decision. In the same chapter of 1 Peter where wives are instructed to submit to their husbands, husbands are told:

> Likewise, ye husbands, dwell with them according to knowledge, giving honour unto the wife, as unto the weaker vessel, and as being heirs together of the grace of life; that your prayers be not hindered. (1 Pet. 3:7)

Surely Rebekah would have told her husband of God's revelation to her about their sons, and the selling of the birthright from Esau to Jacob was most likely a known fact. Moreover, Esau had demonstrated covenant unfaithfulness by taking two wives from the Hittites, and the Scripture calls it a grief to both Isaac and Rebekah (Gen. 26:34–35). Most definitely their prayers were hindered as Isaac was disregarding his wife's counsel, thereby treating her with dishonor and failing to allow her to act as his mirror.

Proverbs 18:22 states, "*Whoso* findeth a wife findeth a good *thing*, and obtaineth favour of the LORD." When Eliezer (Gen. 24) was chosen to find a wife for Isaac, he prayed that God would send to him the woman God had chosen for Isaac. God's providential care in bringing Rebekah to Eliezer is evidence that God had selected Rebekah to be the wife of the patriarch — a selection that served Isaac in good stead.

What About Eve?

Some will argue that part of God's rebuke to Adam after the fall was *because* he listened to the counsel of his wife (Gen. 3:16ff.). Hodge explains:

> The problem was that Eve misunderstood her role. She was to keep her man on target to obey God in all things, not derail him into disobedience against God. Yet this is what she did . . . Similarly, Adam was supposed to listen to his wife — but not when she was mistaken. And on the issue of the forbidden fruit, she was very mistaken.[8]

---

8. Hodge, blog.

Hodge makes the case that Satan approached Eve first *because* of the role God assigned to her. Much the same way that lobbyists will approach (to convince or bribe) a staff member of a legislator to pave the way toward procuring a favorable vote for a particular issue, Satan went to Adam's trusted counselor. He knew that if he could get Eve to accept his propositions, then Adam would have no one to oppose him when he was tempted.[9]

Striking the Balance

The book of Ephesians instructs both husband and wife to understand their relationship as a picture or reflection of Christ's relationship to His church. Each has a particular calling in the marriage: "The submission requirement does not mean she gives up her opposition rights. What it means, is that a wife must learn to oppose the right issues in the right manner."[10]

Here is where we get to the "meat" of the Word. For exercising opposition rights must reflect, by way of analogy, how the church is to submit to Christ. While it is clear that the church does not have the liberty to disobey God's commands, we, as God's creatures, don't always understand or agree with His stated or secret will and we are *encouraged* to petition Him with fervor. (Recall the parables dealing with prayer: The unjust judge *and* the neighbor knocking on his neighbor's door at night are examples to show the people of God how to relate to the Lord in their petitions.) So, too, a wife should carefully choose her opposition for those matters she considers essential to covenantal faithfulness. Her desire to maintain covenantal faithfulness should be exercised with care without destroying the structure of the family. Likewise, her husband should not ignore the petitions of his wife, since God does not ignore the petitions of His church.

In almost four decades of marriage, I have failed in this endeavor more times than I care to enumerate. While my issues had merit, I often overrated the content of my argument and downplayed the

---

9. ibid.
10. ibid.

way I conveyed it. St. Peter admonishes women,

> Likewise, ye wives, be in subjection to your own husbands; that, if any obey not the word, they also may without the word be won by the conversation of the wives; While they behold your chaste conversation coupled with fear. (1 Pet. 3:1–2)

By failing to make "chaste conversation coupled with fear" a top priority, I often sabotaged my own efforts to resolve certain important issues because I failed to hold my tongue or use it wisely. Whether or not I considered that my husband was "fighting fairly," my responsibility was to fear God and keep His commandments (Eccles. 12:13). Peter's instruction is to foster conflict resolution, not to have disagreements buried.

Hodge comments on the "battle of the sexes" in marriage:

> Men do not want to obey God's commandments fully. Wives do not wish to oppose their husbands on these issues, but are more than happy to oppose them on a host of trivial issues. Men now want to rule over their wives, rather than form a formidable team that is a reflection of the relationship between Christ and the church. With the result that too often men are too busy giving orders to take the time to listen to their *'ezer kenegdo.*
>
> There is a challenge, then, for both husbands and wives. Do men fulfill their duty to obey God's commandments? Does a wife see her husband as God sees him, help him identify his true calling under God, and support him in it, opposing him when he strays from the path God has ordained for him? If not, it's time for some changes.[11]

Learning how to be the virtuous, powerful woman of Proverbs 31 takes humility, maturity, and commitment. Knowing the law-word of God sufficiently and practically is essential for a woman who is to look well to the ways of her household. In the end, a man and woman in the partnership of marriage are the building blocks of a godly society, and only when they are willing to sharpen and challenge each other to faithfulness will their efforts bring about a bountiful harvest.

---

11. ibid.

7

The Bible's High Estimation of Women

Those who embrace the law of God as binding on their lives see God's laws as blessings; those who do not, see them as hindrances to their autonomy. God's law acts as a boundary that we move at our peril. By obeying it we are performing our duty before the Lord, (Eccles. 12:13) and we are living a life that is lived according to God's instruction manual.

There are many laws in Scripture that are intended to preserve and enhance the primary institution ordained by God — the family. One is the dowry system. Although greatly maligned and often portrayed as the purchasing of a wife as property, when understood properly, the dowry is evidence of God's intent to build strong families and to protect and cover women.

R. J. Rushdoony notes,

God's law requires a dowry for wives (undowered wives are legally concubines). This gives stability to marriage as an institution. The dowry was normally equal to about three years' wages. A young man did not lightly enter into marriage, nor did he easily abuse his wife; if she then divorced him, he lost the dowry as an inheritance for his children. The abuse of wives was thus costly. Likewise, the wife knew that she could lose the dowry for misconduct and face the anger of her father and brothers. The dowry system thus was a major check on the conduct of both men and women. In a culture given to romantic ideas of marriage, there is no brake on the behavior of husbands and wives, or very little.[1]

Setting the Record Straight

Contrary to revisionist history, it was never the Biblical practice to require that a bride's family pay a dowry to the intended husband in order to get her married. The Biblical position is the opposite. The Bible, having its emphasis on creating strong families, requires that a prospective husband demonstrate to a young woman's father (or uncle or brother in the absence of a father) that he has more than a superficial interest in the daughter. A dowry was among the evidences used to convince a father to release his daughter to the authority and protection of another man. It also showed that the man was a person of integrity and faith.

The book of Genesis presents this practice in numerous places. When Abraham sought a godly woman for his son, Isaac, his servant was sent with a dowry to procure a wife. Her father Bethuel and her brother Laban received Eliezer who plainly stated his mission. The transmission of expensive gifts was a demonstration that Rebekah would be cared for as she left her homeland to marry Isaac.

When Jacob left hurriedly after receiving his birthright, he left without any capital or resources, although his father was wealthy. When he was eager to marry Rachel, he offered seven years of labor to serve as his dowry. Despite the deception of Laban in secretly marrying his older daughter to Jacob, he was acting as a responsible father in making sure his daughters would be cared for. His cheating of the daughters out of their dowries should not be viewed as a negative regarding the dowry system itself. Rushdoony explains,

> In what follows, Laban is commonly abused by commentators. It is true that Laban deceived Jacob, but this is not the whole story. Rebekah had been given a very generous dowry by Eliezer for Isaac; obviously, wealth was in the family. Whatever story Jacob could tell could not erase the fact that he had come with nothing. There was no assurance

1. R. J. Rushdoony, *Genesis* (Vallecito, CA: Ross House Books, 2002), 63.

that, when Jacob returned, his parents might not be dead and Esau in possession of everything. It would have been unwise for any father to entrust his daughter to a man in such a plight. Laban clearly wanted to keep Jacob and his daughters in Haran. His actions were those of a good father. It was his hope that after fourteen years, Jacob would prefer to remain.

It was Jacob who offered to serve Laban seven years as a dowry for Rachel (vv. 19–20). He perhaps reasoned that, after seven years, Esau might be less hostile.[2]

Marriage Is a Covenantal Agreement

Marriage is the picture the Bible uses to show us the relationship of Christ and His bride (the church). The Scriptures tell us that it is Jesus who pursues His bride, arranges the marriage feast, and covers and protects her. When we are justified through His blood, we are given a dowry, the down payment of the Holy Spirit:

> And it is God who establishes us with you in Christ, and has anointed us, and who has also put his seal on us and given us his Spirit in our hearts as a guarantee. (2 Cor. 1:21–22)

In a like manner, the dowry acts as the down payment on the earnestness of the husband in his promise to remain faithful until one of them dies. Why would a woman need such a promise in God's eyes? Because she is the instrument God ordained to carry children into this world and nourish and rear them. Pregnancy and childbearing are vulnerable times for a woman. The husband's prenuptial demonstration of commitment goes a long way in keeping the marriage together because he has shown a willingness to make a significant investment in his new family.

Some argue that this takes the "romance" out of marriage. In actuality, it is quite the contrary. A woman will have a greater sense of her future husband's appreciation of her as a person when he is willing to demonstrate it with the fruits of his labor.[3] What's more, it

---

2. ibid., 203.

3. There are many stories that abound in many cultures of the plain old maid who

demonstrates to her family that this addition to their family brings with him a capability to support her and future children.[4]

The Benefits of an Endowered Wife

The Scripture states that "He who finds a wife finds a good thing, And obtains favor from the Lord (Prov. 18:22)." Finding a wife of good character is an advantage to a man and the Bible tells a man to actively pursue one. Proverbs 31 also describes a worthy woman's price as being "far above rubies." Thus, a prospective husband demonstrates his recognition that he has found a pearl of great price.

When a woman enters a marriage with the resources of a dowry, it gives her the liberty to carry out her calling as wife according to Proverbs 31. She knows that her husband has invested in this marriage before it ever took place and that she is protected against his acting unlawfully towards her, since her family played an integral part in the contractual agreement.

Parents are to play a significant role in the formation of a new family. Their input and direction are another aspect of God's protection of both men and women. Rushdoony states,

> [T]he Hebrew word for bridegroom means "the circumcised," the Hebrew word for father-in-law means *he who performed the operation of circumcision*, and the Hebrew word for mother-in-law is similar. This obviously had no reference to the actual physical rite, since Hebrew males were circumcised on the eighth day. What it meant was that the father-in-law ensured the fact of *spiritual circumcision*, as did the mother-in-law, by making sure of the covenantal status of the groom.

---

everyone expected would never marry, but if she did would only be worthy of one or two cows as the bride-price or dowry. These accounts tell of a rich man who instead of offering the normal number of cows (2–3) instead offered ten cows for this woman. Not only did this alter the view the woman had of herself and caused her beauty to shine forth, but others in her village suddenly had a new found estimation of her. Such is the transformation in a woman when a man truly appreciates her and demonstrates it in practical ways.

4. Whenever a sizable loan is made in procuring land, a house, or a vehicle, the lending institution requires information that shows the person requesting the loan has the means to pay it back. Why should we expect that something of much more value than these should just be entered into with a smile and a promise to be faithful?

It was their duty to prevent a mixed marriage. A man could marry their daughter, and become a bridegroom, only when clearly a man under God.

Thus, the parents of the bridegroom had an obligation to prepare their son for a life of work and growing knowledge and wisdom, and the parents of the bride had a duty, under Biblical standards, to examine the faith and character of the prospective bridegroom.[5]

Rather than have to provide for herself, the dowry acts as the down payment on the continuous provisions that a husband will provide for a woman as she assumes the role of household manager and mother of the children. It should be noted that the dowry is given to the woman's father who holds it in trust for her use and it is not meant to pay for the day to day expenses of the family. The husband is not intended to have access to those resources.[6]

A Father's Role in Protecting His Daughters

The Bible puts a high premium on moral purity and this is tied in to the preservation of the family. That is why adultery is a capital crime. It attacks God's primary institution by breaking the marriage covenant. Additionally, God's law commands that not only a married woman, but also a betrothed woman, is not to be violated either by seduction or rape, and both carry the penalty of death. But the law goes further in that it cites the case of the seduction of an unbetrothed virgin. Rushdoony notes,

> In Deuteronomy 22:25–29, we have the law of rape, but in this instance the word used is "entice." Although the girl participates in the act, the responsibility still rests primarily on the male. In Biblical law, the greater the responsibility the greater the culpability.
>
> Without any qualification whatsoever, the guilty man must pay the virgin "the dowry of virgins." The amount is not specified here, but in

---

5. R. J. Rushdoony, *The Institutes of Biblical Law*, vol. 1 (Phillipsburg, NJ: The Presbyterian & Reformed Publishing, Co., 1973), 344.

6. Contrary to the negative connotations given to prenuptial agreements, the Bible actually prescribes it. And, unlike the community property laws that exist today, the husband was not to maintain control over the dowry given.

Deuteronomy 22:29 we are given the amount, fifty shekels of silver, a very large amount in those days.

This dowry is to be paid whether or not he marries the girl. Seduction was thus too costly to be commonplace in times when the law was kept.

Whether or not a marriage followed depended on the girl's father. If he "utterly refuse" the man as a son-in-law, the dowry still went to the girl. Since a subsequent suitor also paid some kind of dowry, the girl went into her marriage well endowered.

This law stresses the priority of the father over both his daughter and her possible husband. It was his duty to protect his daughter and to ensure a good marriage for her.[7]

While the modern mind rebels against this power given to the father, it should be noted that a godly father has as his primary interest procuring a godly marriage for his daughters. Much more is at stake than the man's personal financial position. The father's goal is to find someone equally trustworthy to himself in the care and protection of his daughter, and one who will be a true covenant head over the new family and children who may follow.

By requiring a dowry from the man who wants his daughter, the father is weeding out those who are not stable and have superficial and temporary designs on the woman.

> This dowry was [the woman's] protection money against abuse or desertion and an inheritance for her children. This dowry system ensured the wife's security and the stability of the family. A man did not readily wrong a wife who held so much family capital, three years' wages normally, in gold or silver.[8]

Guarding a Woman's Reputation

The Bible puts a high premium on being chaste before marriage. This is evidenced in that the dowry amount for a virgin was higher than for a woman who was not. Moreover, the father plays an

---

7. R. J. Rushdoony, *Exodus* (Vallecito, CA: Ross House Books, 2004), 315–316.
8. R. J. Rushdoony, *Numbers* (Vallecito, CA: Ross House Books, 2006), 294.

important role in guaranteeing his daughter's virtue and upholding her honor. A woman's reputation is not only her concern but the concern of her entire family.

Deuteronomy 22:13–21 cites a case law:

> If any man take a wife, and go in unto her, and hate her, And give occasions of speech against her, and bring up an evil name upon her, and say, I took this woman, and when I came to her, I found her not a maid: Then shall the father of the damsel, and her mother, take and bring forth the tokens of the damsel's virginity unto the elders of the city in the gate: And the damsel's father shall say unto the elders, I gave my daughter unto this man to wife, and he hateth her;
>
> And, lo, he hath given occasions of speech against her, saying, I found not thy daughter a maid; and yet these are the tokens of my daughter's virginity. And they shall spread the cloth before the elders of the city. And the elders of that city shall take that man and chastise him; And they shall amerce him in an hundred shekels of silver, and give them unto the father of the damsel, because he hath brought up an evil name upon a virgin of Israel: and she shall be his wife; he may not put her away all his days. But if this thing be true, and the tokens of virginity be not found for the damsel: Then they shall bring out the damsel to the door of her father's house, and the men of her city shall stone her with stones that she die: because she hath wrought folly in Israel, to play the whore in her father's house: so shalt thou put evil away from among you.

Rushdoony has extensive comments on this passage,

> This is not a popular text with feminists because it so clearly gives priority to the family *and* to the parents. The father in particular is seen as centrally important, and the matter of *honor* is stressed.
>
> The seriousness of the matter is seen by the fine cited in v. 19, 100 shekels or weights in silver. In 1 Samuel 9:8 we see that a quarter of a silver shekel was a good gift. A half a shekel was the extent of the poll tax to maintain a civil order (Exod. 30:15; cf. Neh. 10:32). The fine of 100 shekels of silver was virtual confiscation of an estate. (A shekel was a weight of silver, not a coin.) Obviously, the honor of a family and its daughter could not be lightly impugned. This was not the only

penalty. The husband making a false accusation was also to be chastised or beaten (v. 18). To question the honor of a family and its daughter was not something done casually or frequently. The man making the false accusation was not killed because he had to support the wife whose honor he had questioned.

This was to an extensive degree a self-enforcing law. The penalty was such that no man dared question his wife's premarital virtue unless there was certain proof of it. The evidence was not limited to the cloth used when the hymen was broken.[9]

The family is in God's order the basic institution in society. It has priority over church and state. It is man's first and basic government and the primary area of worship and the practice of religion. To undermine the family is to undermine society, a fact well known to our immoralists of today.

There is an important fact about this fine; it is twice as severe as the fine for seduction in vv. 28–29, which is fifty shekels of silver. Deuteronomy 22:28–29 and Exodus 22:16–17 are cognate texts. The payment in Exodus 22:17 is called "the dowry of virgins." From this we can assume that in such cases, as a penalty, the dowry was set somewhat higher than was normally the case. Thus, fifty shekels of silver was a large sum, one equivalent to a total income of perhaps three years, the traditional reckoning of the dowry. This helps us to appreciate the significance of the fine. To defame one's wife deliberately and wrongfully was a very serious offense.[10]

Such is the high value that God's Word places on a woman of the covenant who has remained pure in keeping with the Lord's commandments. The fact that defaming a wife is so costly with both a severe financial penalty and a loss of options for a guilty husband, should debunk the assertion that the Bible subjugates and debases women. By placing such a high regard on the family and its preservation, the law-word of God stands as a condemnation of gender equality and an androgynous culture.

---

9. Commonly referred to as the tokens of virginity, the cloth that was placed on the marriage bed during the first time of intimacy was then given to and safely stored by the woman's father as proof that she was a virgin before marriage.

10. R. J. Rushdoony, *Deuteronomy* (Vallecito, CA: Ross House Books, 2008), 331–332.

In like manner, for the penalty if the husband's charge is true, vv. 20–21 state,

> The wife is executed near the door of her father's house. This is death for the wife and dishonor for her parents. The husband who is guilty of slander lives as the virtual slave of his father-in-law, who now commands his wealth. He remains alive to support his wife and children. The wife who is guilty dies because her duties can be assumed by others.[11]

Rather than a private arrangement between two people that involves none but themselves, the Bible posits the joining of godly covenantal families as the key to dominion in Jesus' name. It is not hard to see that we have seen a systematic removal of all things Biblical from our schools to our courts to our media. Both the Christian family and the church are seen as the great roadblocks to their new world order, and,

> As a result, the legal aspects of family life are trivialized. Since World War II, it has increasingly been the practice to reject substantial reasons for divorce unless a wealth of assets is at stake. Only then will such matters as adultery be considered, and, of late, even in such cases it is waning. If marriage is essentially a private arrangement, this is logical. If it is basic to social order, the present trend is suicidal.[12]

Women Need to Recognize Their Value

Rather than succumbing to the culture that surrounds us, young girls need to embrace their high calling as women. According to Deuteronomy 22:21, a woman who enters into marriage unchaste is said to have "wrought folly in Israel." Rushdoony notes that it amounts to an assault on the social order and is thus treasonous. This bears evidence to the integral part covenantally faithful women play in producing a godly culture. In the case noted, her offense amounts to premarital adultery and shows contempt for both her parents and future husband.[13]

---

11. ibid.
12. ibid.
13. ibid. (I encourage this section to be read in its entirety to get a full appreciation for the deep implications of this law.)

To the modern mind, this case law reeks of a double standard. Not only does the woman lose her life and the man doesn't, but God has placed physical evidences in a woman's body of her infidelity before marriage (broken hymen and/or pregnancy). Some argue that this proves the Bible is misogynistic.

On the contrary, God has protected women in such a way that a woman has the ability not only to prove her virginity (as opposed to a man), but is given tremendous recourse should she be maligned and slandered by her husband. This is God's way of strengthening the family and keeping it intact.

This examination of laws of the Bible that protect women is by no means exhaustive.[14] The people of God need to understand the full counsel of God regarding the basic institution of society — the family — in order to proceed in the building of future covenant families on Biblical terms rather than modern, humanistic ones. When the role of women is viewed in the elevated standards of Scripture, we will see greater evidences of the Kingdom of God in our day.

---

14. This essay has skimmed the surface regarding the provisions within the law of God to preserve and strengthen the family. An extensive study of Rushdoony's commentaries on the Pentateuch and his *Institutes* will do much to enable us to reconstruct this area with greater understanding and authority.

8

Suffering in Silence

Ephesians 5:11 tells us to having nothing to do with the deeds of darkness but to reprove and expose them. Thus, it is not a virtuous act to experience an injustice and let it continue without seeking help or assistance. We need to be (and teach our children to be) people who place a high premium on justice. God's law is an objective one and we should address instances when we have been victims of injustice.

I used to instruct my children that although God's law is most often expressed in the negative, e.g. "Thou shalt not steal," it also conveys the idea none should be silent or approving when someone is stealing from them. Of course, in a society that fails to put God's laws and their penalties into force, it is all too easy to just endure injustice rather than combat it. Infractions against us, in truth, are not primarily against us. When one of God's laws is broken, the offense is first and foremost against Him. That is why it is the responsibility of the person sinned against to seek remedy and not perpetuate the offense (against himself or others) by keeping silent. Anything less leaves doubt that one wasn't victimized but acted in cooperation.

Sadly, there are many "safe" books (ones without foul language, or sexual situations, etc.) that are widely read among young Christian boys and girls that promote the idea of suffering in silence, and elevate such behavior as truly trusting in and being faithful to God. It doesn't take much of an Internet search to discover how many felt wrongly instructed by books such as the *Elsie Dinsmore* series, and how much they resent the "bad advice" they embraced as a result of reading them. One person noted,

> Those books taught me that true godliness was suffering in silence. They taught me that the harshest abuse could be overcome by submitting to God. That cruel, powerful people would eventually become kind if you just gave them more power over you... That God would eventually bring a glorious happy ending to an abusive relationship if you buckled down, numbed/denied/renamed your emotions, [and] guilted yourself for the tiniest rebellion...

This is not the message we want to give our children, and we must be diligent to discuss with them the things they read and flesh out incorrect ideas and conclusions that come from identifying with the hero or heroine of the story.

If we want to see an end to the various injustices that surround us, we must trust that bringing sin out into the open is the correct thing to do. Even though it may feel like one is swimming upstream, the reality is that we must act on principle if we wish to see the tide turned in this regard. And, we need to be found faithfully on the Lord's side when it comes to infractions of His law. His Word tells us, "For nothing is hidden that will not be made manifest, nor is anything secret that will not be known and come to light" (Luke 8:17). As His people, our responsibility is to be a witness to His justice (righteousness), and settle for nothing less.

This is how a Christian society is built!

9

Antinomianism Hurts Women and Children: God's Law Protects Them

High and low-profile cases teem with accounts of women and men being sexually victimized by those in authority over them — by a relative, clergyman, politician, employer, teacher, or Christian ministry leader. Various ministries, organizations, and persons have been blamed for providing a shield for the abusers who commit these sexual crimes against innocent victims.[1]

Similarly, although less well-publicized, there are cases of *false* allegations, usually levied by women against men as payback for supposed wrongs, or as a way to gain sympathy and potential financial reward. In the majority of cases, the burden of producing two witnesses to corroborate or refute the allegations is difficult, given the nature of how sexual scenarios play out.

Such is the sorry state of affairs when Biblical law is not emphasized as the standard for all of life, including human sexual behavior. It is incumbent upon women and men to understand the *demands* of the law regarding human sexuality, in order to serve the Lord faithfully and bring truth to a crooked and perverse generation (Phil. 2:15). The application of God's law is the only remedy when it comes

---

1. Martin Selbrede's article "Liberty from Abuse," in *Faith for All of Life*, Jan/Feb. 2014, focused on the Biblical teaching of shepherds abusing their flocks.

to knowing what sexual behavior is acceptable to God and protecting oneself from victimization by abuse, or protecting oneself against false accusations.

The Battle Rages

Today a battle rages between a *theonomic* view that maintains that God's law speaks to every area of life and thought, and that the social order must be governed by God's law, and the *antinomian* view that maintains that the New Testament overrode the Mosaic law. As a result, the foundations of social order (God's law) have been eroded, and we have seen behaviors that the Bible calls sin declassified into acceptable, natural and even honorable sexual practices.

The church has gone soft on faithful preaching and has reduced most of its teaching to simplistic doctrines that take the teeth out of the Word of God. Rushdoony points out:

> An ancient and persistent danger is the fallacy of simplicity. There is a pronounced resentment on the part of very many men against knowledge that is beyond their capacity. As a result, wherever a democratic impulse governs theology, it seeks the lowest common denominator. The ignorant and foolish piously bleat for "the simple, old-time gospel," when the reality is that their simple-minded gospel is a modern invention. While certain basic doctrines of the Bible are uncomplicated ones, the Bible as a whole is not a simple book, and it gives us no warrant for passing over its complexities to dwell on its simplicities, because both aspects are inseparably one... The demand for simplicity is usually *a demand for perversion*, and it is not surprising, therefore, that the gospel of a democratic era is also a perverted one.[2]

This is all too apparent in most churches today, as shown by the divorce rates among Christians, fornication and adultery among Christians, and the celebration of homosexuality by the majority of "Christian" churches. Rather than preach God's law in matters of sexuality, and adamantly limiting it to the context of heterosexual

---

2. R. J. Rushdoony, *The Foundations of Social Order* (Vallecito, CA: Ross House Books, [1968] 1998), 79.

marriage, the door has been opened to the acceptance of what God calls sexual perversion. Because "thus saith the Lord" has been replaced by "no matter what you do, God will forgive you," a death-wish has befallen the Body of Christ in matters of sexual abuse. Rushdoony continues:

> The demand for simplicity is not only a demand for perversion, but it is also *a demand for suicide*, and the people, church, or institution which pursue it have charted a course for assured death.

Thus a failure to understand and apply God's law has left the church unable to effectively prevent the perversions of the world from invading the church. Sadly, many who present themselves as defenders of the faith are leading the charge against Biblical morality and sexuality.

> Beware of false prophets, who come to you in sheep's clothing but inwardly are ravenous wolves. (Matt. 7:15 NKJV)

Plotting a Course

Proper stewardship of the lives of the children God has given us includes plotting a course of instruction that takes into consideration both our point of origin and our desired destination. Let's examine them in reverse order.

Point of Destination

As Christians, our destination is the Kingdom of God. That is why Christ tells us (Matt. 6:33) to seek first the Kingdom of God and His righteousness. In this context, *first* does not mean the initial step in a series of steps. Rather, the meaning is in terms of *primary* focus — that which should be foremost in our minds and hearts. The only way to obey this command fully is by means of the internal workings of the Holy Spirit driving us to the law of God. The effect of this on our lives and the lives of those who look to us for guidance is to establish the only standard by which we can determine if we are *on course*.

From the earliest interactions with children, God's standard should be referenced and reinforced, keeping in mind that as language develops in the child, so will his understanding. In much the same way that the only reliable assessment of when life begins is at conception, so too, the only reliable assessment of when children can comprehend Biblical truth is *from the beginning*. As I've stated in other places, children are eternal beings in small bodies, and must be viewed and addressed as such. They can understand much more than they can respond to in language.[3]

Teaching the Ten Commandments, the catechism, and Biblical accounts of our forebears in the faith, are all fundamental aspects of what it means "from the time they arise to when they go to bed" (Deut. 6:3–7). And one need not be shy about our family history. There are saints and sinners, to be sure, and our children can learn from their stories. Parents who understand the application of God's law to every area of life and thought, and instruct their children early on, are those who will have "prepared the soil" in which to cultivate godly living.

Teaching Biblical law and its application, and the results for obedience and disobedience, are imperative if we expect children to understand that God's law is a lamp unto their feet in an otherwise very dark environment. Failing to apply Biblical discipline to a child for infractions of God's law is to fail to train up that child in the fear and admonition of the Lord. This is especially true when it comes to the matter of false witness. Our children must understand that if they make an accusation that is later discovered to be false, they will receive the punishment that would have been given to the one falsely accused.

This goes against a "formula approach" to raising one's family — the mindset that says "If we do the right things nothing bad can happen to us. After all, we're Christians." Parents need to establish the law with their children so that when sin rears its ugly head, it can

---

3. Andrea Schwartz, "Eternity in their Hearts" in *Woman of the House* (Vallecito, CA: Chalcedon/Ross House Books, 2012), 69–78.

be dealt with effectively and redemptively. We cannot simply shelter children from "bad things" and expect this to be sufficient. This is a recipe for future problems at best, and disaster at worst. The "real world" needs to be established as the world of God's unchanging law.

Read through the Gospels with your children, stopping to make sure that they understand the circumstances and context as you go. Do the same thing with the Book of Proverbs, not skipping over the references to things you'd rather not talk about. If you feel ill-equipped to handle this, become equipped. Learn as you go. Failure to make the Scriptures understandable and relevant will make them confusing and irrelevant in your children's minds.

Make sure you ask pertinent questions when watching television or films, or as they read through histories or novels: What is the world-view of those who wrote this? What standard is being used to determine right and wrong? What call to action is explicitly or implicitly communicated? This keeps your family on topic when it comes to the Kingdom of God. The best protection for our families is to know and apply God's law as the means by which we "seek first the Kingdom."

Point of Origin

Once a Biblical foundation is laid, acquaint children with *where they are.* This is as important, if not more important, than teaching them their mailing address, phone number, and email address. Parents must teach children their "location" in a society that is actively at war with Christ and His law. Failure to do this abandons your children to a fantasy world where "bad" guys are easily recognized and "good" guys are those who are like them (homeschoolers, Christians, people who participate in the sports they do). This needs to be done in an age-appropriate way, not fostering fear but giving children the proper tools and defenses to maintain their safety.

I recall over thirty years ago when I helped organize a pro-life prayer vigil in the chapel of a local hospital which performed abortions. The vigil was to conclude with a gathering of families, featuring our homeschool children's choir. One of the choir-mothers informed me that her children would not be participating at the gathering because she was sheltering them, waiting to tell them about "abortion and the bomb" (these were her actual words) until they were older. Her children were at least ten years old and most likely already knew about what she thought she had successfully concealed: all this in order to keep them "innocent."

If we fail to make sure our children understand and are able to identify sin (in themselves and others), how will they ever know when someone is sinning against them or when they, themselves, are close to succumbing to temptation? We must teach the normal (e.g., God's requirements for sexuality) before we explain the deviations that they will encounter in a sinful world. We need to do this in an age-appropriate way, and we need to tailor it to each gender in a way that will be meaningful. The important part is that they hear it from their parents first.[4]

Along with this instruction, there needs to be a thorough understanding of what it means to bear false witness and what the Bible says about perjuring oneself (Deut. 19:16–21). A concomitant to not bearing false witness is bearing *true* witness. Without a godly fear of the Lord, children might conceal wrongs done against them or fabricate stories for their own perceived advantage.

For Our Children

In looking back over my own years of growing up, there were a number of times where certain men in authority (a music instructor and my history teacher, to cite two examples) took liberties with me (and I assume with others) because each was reasonably certain I would not say anything to my parents. They were correct; I was sure that my parents would not believe me, as these were not topics we talked about openly.

---

4. My father used to tell the story about his reaction when a classmate in school told him how children came about. He punched the boy stating, "My parents would never do anything like that!" Attempting to keep children "innocent" is not helpful to them in the long run.

These advances were sexual in nature and could have led to a bad situation, but by God's grace the encounters were unpleasant enough that I was able to remove myself from the situations before anything truly untoward took place. In the case of the music instructor, my mother would leave us in the living room during the lesson so that there wouldn't be distractions from my brother and sisters. It was then that the teacher would inappropriately touch me. This made me very uncomfortable, but I remained silent. When the instructor offered to reduce the price of lessons if my mother brought me to his studio, I told my mother that I was no longer interested in learning the guitar. In the case of the history teacher in my all-girls Catholic school, when I would bring forms or papers to the teachers' lounge and no one else was present, he, more than once, kissed me. As a result, I stopped volunteering to be the messenger to the teachers' lounge. Looking back, my silence made it more likely that these men would continue their inappropriate behavior, with others as their victims.

Girls and boys must be taught to value their virginity and know the difference between an accidental touch and those intended to "test the waters." They must be taught to mention immediately to one or both parents any incident, regardless of whether or not they are certain of the motives behind it, or how their reports will be received. They must relate any compromising situation regardless of threats or possible repercussions from their abusers. It should be an established household practice that matters such as these (even if there is some uncertainty) are to be revealed and discussed, and that they will not be dismissed. Then the parents can identify whether an actual offense occurred, giving the child a clear Biblical rationale for their decision.[5] If the parents agree that abuse has occurred, they must develop a plan to protect the child and confront the abuser.

Additionally, children need to be taught God's mandate to value

---

5. Some may argue that this leaves the door open for children to accuse innocent people randomly. However, by teaching that even if people are deceived God will not be mocked, and enforcing Deuteronomy 19:16–21 and the consequence thereof, there is less likelihood of a mentality that says one can lie with impunity.

themselves and their virginity in order to deal with rape or molestation. They should be told to scream out and report the matter, as the Scripture states (Deut. 22:25–28), and to realize that failing to do so calls into question whether or not they were consenting to the activity.[6] The lines of communication must always be open, and they must have certainty that their parents will hold to no other standard than a Biblical one, regardless of the person being accused. In our day, too many are too ashamed to report being raped or sexually molested, especially if it is a person of prominence or authority. They are pressured not to "cry out" by their social environment, often even by their church leaders.

In today's world, we must also instruct our children regarding impure overtures from women or men. We need to help them carry themselves with confidence, but with a healthy discernment in dealing with people. They need to understand the "climate" of the day and realize that they are at a deficit in a culture that magnifies feminism, promiscuity, abortion, and homosexuality. They need to understand also that this is not accidental. In fact, as Rushdoony states:

> In country after country, there are moves to legalize homosexual unions; the laws against homosexuality have been extensively dropped, so that a tacit legality exists. Other perversions are similarly allowed to go unprosecuted. The legal safeguards of the family are increasingly removed, so that again society is threatened with the anarchy of an anti-familistic state and its legalized lawlessness. In the name of equal rights, women are being stripped of the protections of the family and given no place except the perverse competition of a sexual market in which increasingly shock, perversion, deviation, and aggressiveness command a premium. The women who gain by equal rights are those clearly who are hostile to Christian law.
>
> The law, it must be remembered, is warfare against that which is defined as evil and a protection of that which is held to be good. In the developing law structure of humanism, warfare is implicitly waged against the parents and the family as evil, and protection is extended

---

6. Even if a child consents to illicit sexual behavior it doesn't excuse the perpetrator, nor invalidate God's requirements.

to perverts and lawbreakers on the assumption that their "rights" need protecting.[7]

The Treasonous Act of Incest

When modern man thinks of *treason*, the name Benedict Arnold often comes to mind. Here was a man of high military rank in the Continental Army planning to betray those who depended on his leadership and trusted him. Although his plot did not work, his name has forever been linked to betrayal after trust.

In Scripture, certain violations against the family are so significant that they are classified as treason. Rushdoony states,

> [T]he basic institution in Scripture is neither church nor state but rather the family. Because the family is God's basic institution, it is most protected by God's law. The offense of Biblical law in the eyes of many is its strict legislation to protect the family, because treason in Scripture, on the human scene, is to the family, not to the state. The modern concept of treason does not exist in the Bible. Because the family is the basic order of life, God's law guards the life of the family. The family is man's first and basic government, church, school, and vocation . . . The law is addressed to the covenant family, as in Deuteronomy, or in Proverbs. It requires the covenant people of God to establish God's order, beginning in their families.[8]

That is why, when a parent violates, by sexual abuse, a child's trust in the parent, the child is devastated. It is the ultimate betrayal of trust, because children begin life believing that parents are their protectors and defenders. A deep conflict results that often leaves children bewildered and irrational in their actions, feeling the impact of the sin perpetrated against them. This is especially true when this heinous act is done by a parent who professes belief in Jesus Christ as Lord and Savior.[9]

---

7. R. J. Rushdoony, *Institutes of Biblical Law*, vol. 1 (Phillipsburg, NJ: The Presbyterian & Reformed, 1973), 208.

8. R. J. Rushdoony, *In His Service* (Vallecito, CA: Ross House Books, 2009), 23

9. If the Biblical dowry system were in place, a family fractured by sexual sin would

What recourse does a child have in this situation? As society has deviated from God's law and, as the church has agreed in lockstep that God's sanctions no longer apply, the resulting culture is one of injustice rather than Biblical justice with punishment and restitution. If God's penalties were carried out as prescribed in the law for offenses such as preying on children, not only would perpetrators no longer be around to offend again, but those witnessing the penalty would learn that there are quick consequences for crime. The reason given for public executions in the Bible is to "purge the evil from among you" (Deut. 17:7).

Jesus gave a harsh warning to those who would prey upon children:

> But whoever causes one of these little ones who believe in me to sin, it would be better for him to have a great millstone fastened around his neck and to be drowned in the depth of the sea. Woe to the world for temptations to sin! For it is necessary that temptations come, but woe to the one by whom the temptation comes! And if your hand or your foot causes you to sin, cut it off and throw it away. It is better for you to enter life crippled or lame than with two hands or two feet to be thrown into the eternal fire. And if your eye causes you to sin, tear it out and throw it away. It is better for you to enter life with one eye than with two eyes to be thrown into the hell of fire.
>
> See that you do not despise one of these little ones. For I tell you that in heaven their angels always see the face of my Father who is in heaven. What do you think? If a man has a hundred sheep, and one of them has gone astray, does he not leave the ninety-nine on the mountains and go in search of the one that went astray? And if he finds it, truly, I say to you, he rejoices over it more than over the ninety-nine that never went astray. So it is not the will of my Father who is in heaven that one of these little ones should perish. (Matt. 18:6–14 ESV)

With this in mind, teaching God's commandments in the family and from the pulpit is a necessity. Families meeting regularly in congregations of the *faithful* become a safeguard and protection from deviant behaviors. Interestingly, right after the passage quoted above,

---

have the resources to move forward without having to rely on the offending spouse/parent.

Jesus establishes the well-known Matthew 18 protocol. Children should be taught early on that the Matthew 18 protocol is open to them, and they should have the assurance that those in the church will investigate and help them in their time of need.

The goal of keeping children "innocent" is a misplaced one. Our goal is to help our children to live righteously. If they are not adequately prepared for the practical applications of what that means in the age in which they live, we are setting them up for potential injury, physical, mental, and spiritual.

10

Self-Defense from a Biblical Perspective

The only time I have had a black eye was in 1991 during my second-degree brown belt promotion test in Kenpo Karate. These rites of passage included a vigorous two-plus-hour ordeal where the candidate for advancement had to demonstrate proficiency in the various moves from previous belt levels. Additionally, one also had to withstand simulated attacks from the men who were black belts who ran the test. My "shiner" resulted when I did not deflect an incoming punch in a timely manner.

By this time, I had been studying martial arts for six years, yet this was my first experience with a full punch to the face. That was a remarkable record considering I was thirty-seven years old at the time. You see, girls do not customarily fistfight when they are at odds with each other; rather, they give way to pulling hair and kicking. Surprisingly, the blow to my face was not as bad as I had imagined one would be. With the adrenalin rush, I was able to successfully complete the process and pass the test!

I attribute this accomplishment, in part, to my hard work and physical conditioning, but also because of the reason I pursued proficiency in self-defense in the first place. As a Christian, I knew there were priorities set forth in Scripture that required that I prepare myself to maneuver through a sinful world.

Since then, I have combined my knowledge of God's Word with the techniques and perspectives I gained through martial arts to present seminars to women highlighting self-defense from a Christian/Biblical perspective. I begin these seminars by pointing out that three of the Ten Commandments (the sixth, seventh, and eighth) are pertinent to this discussion.

The Morality of Self-Defense

Since it is wrong to kill, failing to defend our life or the life of another violates the sixth commandment. Since adultery (and all fornication) is prohibited, women must value their marriage (or future one) enough to protect themselves in keeping with the seventh commandment. In addition, theft of any kind (including one's virginity, chastity, and purity) appropriately deserves opposition based on the eighth commandment.

This flies in the face of many recommendations given to women either explicitly or implicitly by our modern culture. Too often, women are instructed to cooperate with an assailant to avoid being killed. This avoids the fact that God's penalty for rape and kidnapping is the same as for murder — death. Therefore, it is faulty reasoning to assume that preserving one's life is the utmost priority. Because women are vulnerable to physical and sexual attacks due to the disparity between the strength and size of men and women, it is important for women to follow the dictates of God's Word in Proverbs 31:17, "She girds herself with strength, And strengthens her arms." The Bible does not call for flimsy, weak women. Strength of character and physical strength are both to be pursued. By standing firmly on a Biblical worldview, a woman can prepare herself to be ready to respond in the case of threatening situations.

Unlike the modern recommendation to cooperate with an assailant, the Bible requires that a woman cry out in the case of a sexual assault. In fact, she should do so in order to dismiss any doubt that she is a willing participant. The only time this is not required is when the assault is taking place in a location where she cannot be heard. This does not preclude her crying out; rather, it makes allowance for the fact that her cries would not be effective (Deut. 22:25–28).

Judd Wilson, a military veteran, addresses this passage in his essay, "The Biblical Duty of Self-Defense":

> I have a wife and a tiny, infant daughter. Those women are the most important people on this planet to me. Like other Christian men, I have been commanded by God to love my wife as Christ loves His church and to raise my daughter in the fear and admonition of the Lord. But in the face of a palpable silence in the evangelical world regarding this subject, I pose a question. Do I not have the duty to protect them from physical harm?
>
> The Bible says, "Thou shalt not tempt the Lord thy God" (Matt. 4:7). Citing this verse, the Lord refused Satan's call to recklessly jump off the temple, and in so doing to deny Biblical common sense in favor of supernatural deliverance. If I send my wife and daughter to the grocery store, the grandparents' house, or anywhere else, unprepared to deal with this world full of scheming, depraved sinners, have I not broken this commandment?
>
> I'm not saying that we should discount God's protection and blessing or the customary decency of many citizens; but if I neglected to check the oil, the gas, and the tires before setting out on a road trip, would I not be to blame if we ended up stranded on the side of a road somewhere? I must conclude then that I have a duty to prepare my girls to defend themselves and that I must be able to defend myself as well.[1]

Some may argue that Deuteronomy 22:25–28 is antiquated and does not reflect modern life. They submit that there are circumstances whereby a woman is tricked or manipulated into compromising situations by a person who is powerful and who may discredit her account. This is why the other admonitions in Scripture regarding modesty, prudence, integrity, and remaining under the care and protection of family are so important. Instead of making this an issue of women's rights and the double standard that exists in humanistic culture, the Bible calls for women to cherish their bodies as temples of the Holy Spirit and protect their sexuality in a preemptive way. As the saying goes, "An ounce of prevention is worth a pound of cure."

---

1. www.chalcedon.edu/faith-for-all-of-life/theocracy-now/the-biblical-duty-of-self-defense

Today it is standard practice to move outside the protection and covering of one's family and blithely assume that bad things should not happen to good people. Coupled with the low priority often given to modesty and godliness, females leave the door open to be disbelieved and challenged when there is a charge of rape or abuse. Regardless of whether or not it *should* be this way, the credibility of a woman who fornicates when she chooses to do so, and then expects allegations of rape to be believed unquestionably, will be called into question. Proverbs 20:11 tells us, "Even a child makes himself known by his acts, by whether his conduct is pure and upright." In a like manner, the character of a godly woman should be so well known, that her words are taken seriously and her testimony believed.[2]

Many passages in the Bible advise that avoiding certain behaviors is a protection against the wickedness that exists in the world. What often seems like prudery or overprotectiveness to the young person who wants to experience excitement in life is in actuality God's safeguard. This does not mean that women should not pursue education, employment, or activities outside the home. Rather, it is a prescription for doing all these things under the protection and covering of her family. Only the fool has to learn everything by personal experience. Therefore, adhering to the guidelines of the Creator is more than commendable; it is vital.

Once this perspective is embraced, the process of learning how to defend oneself is the next priority. Good physical conditioning gives opportunity to escape from a perpetrator and/or dangerous environment should the situation arise. Often this is all that is needed. Being weak and lethargic due to excessive weight or muscular weakness makes a woman more likely to be taken advantage of. Being physically fit is not anathema to femininity. When a woman is in better physical health and carries herself with godly deportment, she makes herself a less vulnerable target.

Good instruction as to how to defend oneself is available all over

---

2. Teaching and applying the Biblical teaching that perjurers (those who give false testimony) are subject to whatever punishments that would be levied against those they accuse, would lessen false accusations.

the internet, and various videos and articles abound about effective means to ward off an attacker. While it is good to get some hands-on training, there is much to be learned by educating yourself online. This is also an effective way for parents to train both daughters and sons to be able to be pro-active in this area.[3]

Problems under the Radar

Along with learning that being punched in the face was not as bad as I had anticipated, I also learned how uncomfortable people were even to broach the subject with me when they saw me at church or at homeschool gatherings. In fact, their discomfort was palpable and almost funny. No one wanted to ask the obvious question, "What happened to you?" I must admit that I relished seeing how proficient they were at avoiding the "elephant in the room." Since I was not ashamed of my "shiner," I did not attempt to conceal it with makeup. The only people who would confront me head-on were children who would ask unapologetically, "What happened to your eye?"

This brings me to the unpleasant subject of sexual or physical misconduct/abuse on the part of one spouse to another, or a parent to a child. One does not have to look very far to learn of the tragic stories of people who endured years of being taken advantage of by someone they trusted. The question arises: Why did these occurrences remain secret? What social norms existed within the circles that gave precedence to exchanging niceties over unearthing real problems within their midst? Why aren't these subjects broached from the pulpit?

Judd Wilson goes on to note:

> We read about this duty of self-defense in Deuteronomy 22:23–27, which teaches us that when threatened with rape, a woman has the obligation to resist her attacker by screaming for help. The principle implicit here is that this crime is something to be resisted, not acquiesced to. Verses 23–24 mention the case of a woman who is attacked while in a town. It specifies that if she does not scream for help, she is

---

3. There are also many classes available throughout most communities. Be sure to check that your instructors are competent and certified in the techniques they teach.

to be stoned to death along with the rapist. Why? *Because she is obliged to resist.* [Emphasis mine.]

This is not the law of some cruel and unjust God; it is the law of a God who sharply differentiates between good and evil. As Matthew Henry writes on these verses, the assumption here is that in a town or other populated area, when a woman cried out for help, rescuers "might speedily have come in to prevent the injury offered her." In the case of a sexual assault, that help must be immediate. We can conclude, then, that Israelite city dwellers were not to be couch potatoes, but instead vigilant, manly individuals capable of physically overcoming a criminal or a group of criminals.

Verses 25–27 specify that in the case of a woman raped in the countryside, where there is no one to hear her cry for help, only the rapist must die, for "as when a man riseth against his neighbour, and slayeth him, even so is this matter: For he found her in the field, and the betrothed damsel cried, and there was none to save her." Again, *the woman is obligated to resist,* [emphasis mine] and her fellow Israelites are obligated to rescue her. We also see that the Israelites were expected to know how to help her. Clearly a girl today, just as then, is better off knowing how to defend herself if she is caught alone with "no one to rescue her."[4]

One of the safeguards of the Bible's directive for a woman to cry out is that it puts the offender on notice. Too many, unaware of this aspect of the law-word of God, tragically felt they had to endure vile treatment from a family member or trusted friend, feeling personal shame and guilt. This is why learning Biblical law is a priority: it serves as a protection and shield. Such knowledgeable application may not prevent a first offense, but certainly would avert repeated ones. Thus, the command for a woman to cry out and pursue justice goes beyond the occurrence of the actual attack. It means a speedy reporting to those who can help her, rather than concealing the offense for years. Moreover, as Judd Wilson points out, the congregation was expected to know how to help her.

Regardless of the "good reasons" to avoid letting someone know

---

4. ibid.

that a violation has taken place (threats of retaliation or accusations of lying), knowing that one is acting in obedience to God's law provides strength. Also knowing that there are people ready, willing, and able to help encourages openness. When we are told to seek first the Kingdom of God and His righteousness, it is important to note that the words "righteousness" and "justice" are synonymous. We have a duty to see that justice is served, but it cannot be a solo effort. An aspect of God's establishing the institutions of both church and state was and is to serve as protection for the family in its Kingdom work. Pride, scarred reputations, or potentially bad press are not sufficient excuses to sacrifice justice.

Too many church people embrace a culture of superficiality, priding themselves in minding their own business to avoid being labelled busybodies. This flies in the face of the passage in Galatians that instructs us to bear one another's burdens as the fulfillment of the law of Christ (Gal. 6:2). The body of Christ must do more than decry the bad behavior of the heathen; we must deal with the wolves that maintain free access within churches with members who value politeness over community.

The entire subject of self-defense opens the door to discussion about important and pertinent issues of our day. Rather than merely shielding ourselves and our children from the sinful, humanistic culture surrounding us, and its infiltration into our churches, we should be establishing a firm Biblical foundation of a godly, dominion-oriented response to these issues. Prioritizing the clear commands and boundaries of Scripture, and carrying them out, will do much to avoid unnecessary suffering.

> The prudent sees danger and hides himself, but the simple go on and suffer for it. (Prov. 22:3)

II

Moving the Ancient Boundaries

Mankind has always been faced with a choice: either accept God's terms (and His definitions of terms), or construct independent and self-serving ones. When a culture constructs new ways of referring to Biblical concepts, it is evidence that it is in active rebellion against God and its laws and conduct will reflect such rebellion. When the people of God succumb to altered definitions and modern adjustments to God's Word, the results are detrimental and decidedly wicked. What's more, issues that are clear-cut in the Bible and clearly defined in Scripture become muddied and unnecessarily complex.

In the law of God as given to Moses and fulfilled (put into force) by Christ, certain behaviors are deemed capital offenses. This means that God requires the death penalty to be imposed by the civil government on people who commit these crimes. In addition to the justice demanded by God for these crimes, the death penalty also purges evil from among the people. Yet in our day and age, due to antinomian compromise within the church and outright humanism in the secular world, we have replaced Biblical terms with euphemistic ones and compounded the problem by inserting the concept of "mitigating circumstances" to areas where the Scripture speaks plainly and clearly.

An example of this is the term "fornication." In Scripture this refers to and umbrellas any sexual behavior that is outside the bounds of godly, covenant marriage between a man and a woman. R. J. Rushdoony notes,

In Proverbs, all extra-marital sexuality is condemned, and the counsels concerning the evils of prostitution, adultery, and premarital sexuality are all given as age-old wisdom and implicit in God's law. Marital chastity is declared to be the standard (Prov. 5:1–23). It is presented, not as an impoverishing life, but as a well-spring of joy and health to man's being.[1]

Some like to posit a different set of rules under the New Covenant. There is no Biblical basis for this antinomian perspective,

> The New Testament forbad all non-marital sexual intercourse, and pre-marital relations therefore as well, without any concern other than to restate the Biblical law for Greek and Roman converts (Acts 15:20, 29; 21:25; Rom. 1:29, 1 Cor. 5:1; 6:13, 18; 7:2). Christ forbad the thoughts leading to it (Matt. 5:28).
>
> Clearly then, Biblical law is designed to create a familistic society, and the central social offense is to strike at the life of the family. Adultery is thus placed on the same level as murder, in that it is a murderous act against the central social institution of a healthy culture.[2]

As adultery requires the death penalty under God's law, so too do other specific acts of fornication: rape, homosexuality, and incest. But today these transgressions of the law are given euphemisms in our modern culture. Adultery is sanitized to "having an affair." Rape has lost much of its meaning due to promiscuity being the norm rather than the exception, not to mention how in some circles, any act of sex between a man and a woman is deemed rape depending on the mindset of the woman.[3] And, words such as "gay" and "queer" have replaced the term homosexual that is used in Scripture. Parents or parent-figures are said to have molested or abused their children — terms not found in Scripture — rather than having committed

---

1. R. J. Rushdoony, *Institutes of Biblical Law* (Phillipsburg, NJ: The Presbyterian & Reformed Publishing Company, 1973), 395.

2. ibid.

3. Reducing fornication to a "matter of personal choice" rather than an infraction of God's law makes the entire subject of discerning actual rape a difficult one. That said, humanistic definitions and perspectives rarely result in outcomes that reflect justice, as in the case of Potiphar's wife and her false accusation against Joseph.

incest with them and by extension adultery against their spouse if they are married. Add to this the societal conditioning, where perjury is expected, yet rarely prosecuted, not to mention that the death penalty is all but extinct. Is it any wonder that within and without the church there seems to be no end of the reports of gross sexual misconduct? In truth, the people of God often prove helpless in separating the fact from the fiction and have no inkling as to how to apply God's law to these situations.

Martin Selbrede notes that for certain transgressions of God's law (covered under the term "abuse"), "Any number more than zero is one too many."[4] He states,

> There are as many kinds of abuse as there are sinful impulses in the heart of man. Physical, emotional, spiritual, sexual, and ecclesiastical abuse must never be depersonalized or smeared with the vocabulary of collusion. Where abuse has in fact occurred, it must be dealt with in a godly way. Ezekiel 34 can help us grasp the manifold facets of such abuse and harm that can be inflicted on one or more sheep . . .
>
> [I]f we fail to take God's oath seriously, and move to retain individuals in capacities where the harm they inflicted can be repeated, we will have placed ourselves firmly on the side of injustice. Small wonder that the modern church is filled with the walking wounded . . . Deuteronomy 16:20 reads "Justice, justice shalt thou do," not "Injustice, injustice shalt thou preserve and protect."[5]

Since the operative nature of God's law is ignored by most people and churches, and is not customarily the subject of Sunday sermons, it is easy to let standards other than Biblical ones rule the day. Uninformed or partially informed comments on social media often determine the guilt or innocence of the accused or accuser. Emotionalism and slander replace solid Biblical thinking. Even those who claim to adhere to theonomic principles are likely to abandon them in order to spare themselves or their congregations embarrassment or condemnation.

If we are serious about wanting to protect children, women, and

---

4. Martin Selbrede, "Liberty from Abuse," *Faith for All of Life* Jan/Feb 2014.
5. ibid.

society from sexual predators, we need to teach children (at home and in church) from the earliest age what God has to say on the subject of lawful sexuality. Some will protest that this instruction will sexualize children prematurely, but failing to teach them leaves them fair game for perpetrators and aggressors. Better that they become acquainted with these matters from those who will provide instruction from a thoroughly Biblical perspective, than from someone without the same interest and concern for them.

It is always preferable to provide instruction before problems arise when the terms and context of the teaching can be done calmly and systematically. Those whose families have been ravaged by sexual violations often agree with this statement in hindsight. Although the following examples are hardly of the same magnitude of teaching children how to obey God in the area of sexuality, they illustrate the point that we regularly address the reality of potentially negative outcomes as we prepare our children for scenarios they may encounter.

- When a family is planning a wilderness vacation or a simple hike, instruction is given to children to be on the lookout for poison ivy and poison oak. The plants are described and they are schooled in how to spot them before they are standing in the midst of them. One could argue that by pointing these out to children ahead of time they will go and seek out the plants and play there. However, by calling their attention to the hazards posed by even touching them, unnecessary pain and suffering can be avoided.
- When teaching young people to drive, we encourage the concept of defensive driving. By demonstrating the devastating effects of collision injuries or even death, and encouraging the frequent and proper use of mirrors, speed limits, and safe driving practices, we help a new driver maneuver through the hazards associated with getting behind the wheel. Rarely do these precautions dissuade the teen from driving altogether. Just the opposite is the case. The person is better equipped to deal with the inevitable challenges that will be faced each time he assumes the role of a driver.

While Their Hearts Are Tender

Very young children are often the target of sexual predators (both within and without the church). Their trusting natures and their eagerness to please give an advantage to those who seek to harm them. We do not have to "toughen" the tender hearts of children to prevent them from becoming victims. We can speak to their tender hearts as we teach God's rules and show that God's laws are operative even for children. So, as we instruct children on modesty (not running around without clothes on), and respecting the personal spaces and the bodies of others (not solving their differences by coming to blows), we can also teach that because of God's high premium on marriage and fidelity, care must be taken to remain in His will long before a person is ready for marriage.

Discussing why we cover certain parts of our body and guard our chastity is a way sin (the opposite of godliness) and its effects can be explained to children. If you teach them when they are young, they have the principle in place before they experience temptation in these areas. If they understand that mommy and daddy have an exclusive relationship with each other that does not include other people, and that the same rules apply to them even before they marry, red flags will go up if something contrary to Biblical teaching is offered to them.

Because of the epidemic of adults fornicating with children, it is important that we refine our terms so that gullible children are not fooled by "friendly" people who come bearing treats or presents. The familiar admonition, "Don't talk with strangers," implies that the only true threats come from people they don't know. However, once someone has been introduced and seen on a regular basis, the designation of stranger no longer applies. Instead, children should be told that secrecy from their parents is never an acceptable condition when dealing with others. Someone who wishes to take advantage of children will usually encourage secrecy and instruct them not to speak to others about any of what takes place. Whether they are seduced by pleasure or intimidated by fear, if children have not been prepared to recognize a sinful situation, defend themselves, and report it to their parents, then their vulnerability is a direct result of parental negligence, at best.

In the devastating scenario of a parent abusing his or her own son or daughter, the non-offending parent must remember that Biblically the responsibility and loyalty is first and foremost to God, and then to protect the child. Attempting to handle revelations of sexual misconduct privately and without outside assistance compounds the problem and makes discovering the truth or falsity of the claim additionally difficult.

Biblical definitions and Biblical consequences must be taught and understood if we hope to bring light to this very dark area. We must use the Biblical terms for these specific acts of fornication: adultery, incest, rape, and homosexuality. Trying to soften these terms only serves to lessen the fact that the acts are primarily offenses against God, and that His Word contains the consequences for so doing.

Among the problems attendant with this entire subject is the absence of Biblical terms to replace the concepts of *abuse* and *molestation*. As we've moved away from Biblical definitions, the waters get muddier and muddier. Moreover, some want to dismiss any allegation by a child or teen if there are no corroborating witnesses.[6] While it is true that it takes wisdom to adjudicate in these matters,[7] without people who place God's law above personal considerations or public opinion, we don't have a fighting chance.

The Bible is not silent regarding those who don't have corroborating witnesses to sexual offenses perpetrated against them. Psalm 10:2–11 describes the plea of the oppressed person. Most definitely, those who are victimized by the sexual aggression of others fall into the category of the oppressed. Note how well the psalmist describes the actions of the wicked as they go after the weak and helpless.

---

6. Making use of a rape kit, along with a medical exam, in the case of sexual penetration, can serve as corroborating testimony.

7. See 1 Kings 3:16-18. King Solomon did not have the benefit of the testimony of two witnesses who agreed with one another. His knowledge of the law and experience applying it was such that he was granted wisdom when it came to determining which of the two harlots was telling the truth.

2. In arrogance the wicked hotly pursue the poor; let them be caught in the schemes that they have devised.

3. For the wicked boasts of the desires of his soul, and the one greedy for gain curses and renounces the LORD.

4. In the pride of his face the wicked does not seek him; all his thoughts are, "There is no God."

5. His ways prosper at all times; your judgments are on high, out of his sight; as for all his foes, he puffs at them.

6. He says in his heart, "I shall not be moved; throughout all generations I shall not meet adversity."

7. His mouth is filled with cursing and deceit and oppression; under his tongue are mischief and iniquity.

8. He sits in ambush in the villages; in hiding places he murders the innocent. His eyes stealthily watch for the helpless;

9. He lurks in ambush like a lion in his thicket; he lurks that he may seize the poor; he seizes the poor when he draws him into his net.

10. The helpless are crushed, sink down, and fall by his might.

11. He says in his heart, "God has forgotten, he has hidden his face, he will never see it."

Proper Jurisdiction

Failing to acquaint children with the tactics and strategies of those who might oppress them leaves them at a decided disadvantage when it comes to protection. We must insist that our children tell us immediately of anything untoward that happens to them. This policy protects both the accused and the accuser so that steps can be taken to investigate the matter and bring in the civil authorities to help adjudicate the truth or falsehood of the claims. Anything less subverts justice (one way or the other) and creates a shadow-world of secrecy.

Some object to calling in civil authorities, stating that the ungodly status quo disqualifies the civil realm from dealing with such accusations and crimes. This argument fails on many counts, not the least of which is the God-given jurisdiction for justice God gives to the state. If we are going to call into question instances of overreach by one institution into the affairs of others (health, education, and welfare), we must uphold the proper duties of the civil magistrate.

Others call it a matter for the church to deal with. This, again, fails because the church does not wield the sword and for this reason must bring in civil authorities to determine whether allegations of sexual violation have occurred. The church has the power of excommunication, which may be in order for the offender, but that in and of itself does not bring about justice for the offended. We must make proper use of the institution God has ordained to deal with such matters, even if it exercises its role imperfectly. This should be the impetus for God's people to work toward the Christian reconstruction of society so that we end up with a godly civil realm.[8]

Liability of the Bystander

Along with training children to be forthright with their parents (or another adult in the case of an offending parent), the person who becomes aware of the situation of sexual violation has a responsibility to aid the afflicted. Rushdoony notes,

> [T]his principle of responsibility appears in Deuteronomy 22:24. A woman assaulted in a city is presumed to have given consent if she does not raise a cry, the origin of the *hue and cry* common law. At her cry, every man within sound of her voice has a duty to render immediate aid; failure to do so was regarded as a fearful abomination which polluted the land, and figuratively, darkened the sun.[9]

Not unlike in the man in the parable of the Good Samaritan, we must render aid when we are approached by an oppressed or afflicted person. We cannot fall back on the fact that we're too busy or we are uncertain as to the truth or falsity of the claim. We are not to be a bystander to the situation, but must help to bring about justice. Again Rushdoony comments,

---

8. Just as in the circumstance of a fire in your home, or evidence of an intruder breaking a window in the middle of the night, the first call that will be made is to the fire department or the police, rather than your elders. Not that your elders might not be called in, too; but their help and support fall into a different category.

9. R. J. Rushdoony, *Institutes of Biblical Law*, 464.

The civil legal situation may be an equivocal one; the Biblical legal requirement is not. Misprision, i.e., the concealment of a crime, is a serious offense. The inactive bystander is a party to the crime. The parable of the Good Samaritan (Luke 10:29–37) was firmly based on Biblical law.

In the parable of the Good Samaritan, the priest and the Levite avoided the victim and "passed by on the other side." The religious leaders claimed to obey the law; they tithed "mint and rue and all manner of herbs, and pass over judgment and the love of God" (Luke 11:42). It was an easy matter to tithe mint; it sometimes required moral courage to help a victim; in the case of the victim Jesus described, not even courage was required, only assistance in terms of the law to a victim abandoned by the criminals. The religious leaders kept the law only when it cost them little or nothing to do so. Jesus confounded them from the law.

It is thus a serious error to reduce the parable of the Good Samaritan to the level of feeling alone, or to a matter of charity; these things are subordinate to the law in this case. Those who despise the law are also without charity. They profess to love the law, but they choose simple matters for obedience and despise the things which are difficult. Too many churchmen today reduce the law to simple rules about the sabbath and adultery and bypass or violate the rest of the law with impunity. This is Pharisaism.[10]

Although no one enjoys conflict, there are times when unpleasant accusations need to be dealt with scripturally. Unless the people of God adhere to God's Word in the area of sexuality, they will not be able to deal with the ugly situations that a wicked and perverse generation presents us with. We represent Christ as Christians and need to understand that the psalmist is calling *us* to insist on justice — justice on God's terms.

O Lord, you hear the desire of the afflicted; you will strengthen their heart; you will incline your ear to do justice to the fatherless and the oppressed, so that man who is of the earth may strike terror no more. (Ps. 10:17–18)

---

10. ibid., 467.

12

The Role of Mothers in Building a Kingdom-Driven Family

I dedicated my most recent book: *A House for God: Building a Kingdom-Driven Family* to my husband with these words:

> To Ford, who relentlessly encourages me to boldly pursue the Kingdom of God. And although at times I'm sure I'm a handful to deal with, without his leadership, encouragement, and patience, pursuing my calling under God would be severely limited.

I am the mother of three grown children, and the grandmother of three. I have written a number of books that were inspired by my experiences as mother and educator for over twenty-eight years. When I ran out of children to teach, I answered God's call to share what I knew and had learned with other wives and mothers. That is what occupies a good part of my life these days.

I had the pleasure of knowing Dr. Rushdoony from 1985 till the time of his death in 2001. However, my relationship with him began earlier when I first read the *Institutes of Biblical Law*. As a result of going through that book, Rushdoony became a trusted advisor long before I met him in person. Subsequently, I've read almost everything he has written. I began working for Chalcedon as a volunteer and am currently an employee of the Chalcedon Foundation. In the thirteen years since I last spoke to him, I have continued my relationship with him by listening to his sermons and reading and often re-reading what he wrote. His books continue to be a source of valuable wisdom to me and I use them in my teaching and regularly recommend them to others.

I recall one conversation I had with him. A pastor asked me to ask Rush the following question: How would you describe Christian Reconstruction in a couple of sentences? Well, Rush didn't need a couple of sentences. He answered with one: *Reading the Scriptures as though every verse was written for you and applies to you.*

I've carried this perspective as I read and apply the law-word of God (as Rush would call it) to myself as an individual and also in my joint-calling as wife, mother, and grandmother. And, at the encouragement of Dr. Rushdoony's wife, Dorothy, I assumed the role of the "older woman" as described by Titus 2, making it a priority *to be a teacher of good things; to teach the young women to be sober, to love their husbands, to love their children, To be discreet, chaste, keepers at home, good, obedient to their own husbands, that the word of God be not blasphemed.*

Our subject today is the role of wives and mothers in building a Kingdom-driven family.

First, I will define my terms so that you know what I mean when I say Kingdom-driven. When I speak of the Kingdom, I mean the realm of the King of kings and Lord of lords — Jesus Christ. I mean every square inch, not only of the physical world, but the world of thought, emotion, spirit, and my entire soul, strength, and might. After all, Jesus told us that we are to make a primary focus of our day-to-day lives the Kingdom of God and His righteousness. I submit that fulfilling that command is impossible if God's law-word is not embraced as the standard of righteousness, or its synonym, justice.

Wife is easy to define — the covenanted partner of a husband.

Mother: the person, either by biology or through adoption, who is given the responsibility and privilege of raising children.

To be specific, wife and mother are gender specific terms, and no matter how anyone tries to twist them, they are roles assigned to women. Likewise, the terms daughter and sister are gender specific, and when a female interacts with the words of the Bible, she must interpret them in terms of the roles given her by the Creator. It would be faulty to assume that when I speak of these roles that I am referring to many of the stereotypes presented from the left, the right, and within Christian circles. But more about that later.

Finally, family is defined as the primary institution and social group — both in terms of creation and in terms of priority — within which mankind is to operate. The parents are father and mother — not father and father or mother and mother — they are gender specific roles that are governed in the creation/dominion mandate. Rushdoony notes:

> The sexual character of men and women is not a blind and accidental product of evolution but the purpose of God and basic to any understanding of man. Attempts to deny the validity of Biblical sexual regulations, to read homosexuality as an expression of a primitive development or as another form of man's free sexual expression, or to deny the psychological differences between a man and a woman, are thus morally as well as psychologically wrong. The facts of maleness and femaleness are basic and constitutive of God's purpose for mankind, and any psychology which denies them is thereby sterile and void of understanding. Ironically, the humanists, who condemn Biblical standards as puritanical and inhibited, are themselves guilty of the worst inhibitions in their denial of sexual differences and their psychological validity. The equalitarianism of humanistic psychologies works towards a basic castration of the sexual nature of man and woman and is a major force in modern society.[1]

The family model in Scripture is not the atomistic family: dad, mom, and the kids, or the extended family, throwing in a few grandparents, aunts, and uncles here and there. The Biblical model is the trustee family, with emphasis on health, education, and welfare of the family being maintained by a network of relatives. Because the church did not teach and maintain this Biblical emphasis, it opened the door to the nanny state.

---

1. R. J. Rushdoony, *Revolt Against Maturity* (Vallecito, CA: Ross House Books, 1987), 10.

Within these definitions, I will explore the vital role that the wife and mother plays in the building of a Kingdom-driven trustee family.

As I was preparing this talk, I was concerned that the men, who will never be wives and mothers, would not be interested in what I have to say on this subject. Will they view it as just a talk for women? Will husbands say, "I sure hope my wife gets something out of this talk"?

Or how about the unmarried men? Will this be a time to check their email or see how their favorite baseball team is faring? Or how about the unmarried women? If they are yet to become wives and mothers, will they feel that they are not a part of my targeted audience — wives and mothers?

I expressed this concern to Ford, and he assured me that anyone who takes God's command to seek the Kingdom seriously should most decidedly be interested in this topic because

- Men were never intended to pursue dominion apart from having the assistance of a wife. So, for the married man, it is profitable for him to understand what his other half can and should be doing.
- For the unmarried men listening, they should be keenly interested in the Scriptural demands for being a wife and mother in order to pursue a qualified candidate and make a righteous selection.
- For unmarried women, becoming expert in applying God's Word will make them better able to step into a godly and fulfilling marriage to a man they can honestly submit to.

So, he reassured me this was not just for the ladies.

The book of beginnings (the Book of Genesis) lays the groundwork for building a Kingdom-driven family by identifying God's purpose for creating man. God created mankind for dominion under Him. God had Adam establish himself in his dominion work of tilling the garden and classifying the animals to allow him to understand what the focus of his life should be — God-ordained work.

Rushdoony points out in *Revolt Against Maturity*,

The exercise of dominion under God is the development of man and the earth by means of work in order to strengthen, prosper, and heighten man's life and service under God. True work and true dominion further life and the potentialities of life.[2]

In the process, God was willing for Adam to experience his calling and come to understand there was a void in his life. Have you ever asked yourself why the first "not-good" of the Bible was God saying there was need for a woman? God stating that it is not good for man to be alone? Why did God wait for Adam to realize that none of the animals would serve as a suitable helper for him before he was given a wife? I think it is safe to say that God didn't want Adam to be a loner in his task for dominion. And, although God could have propagated the race with some sort of cloning mechanism, He determined that offspring would proceed from the bone of Adam's bone and the flesh of Adam's flesh.

Based on this, I can unabashedly say that the foremost calling for me as a woman is to help my husband in his dominion calling, i.e., in his work, and, as part of that assistance, bear him children and nurture them in the fear and admonition of the Lord. As a wife and mother, my role is to read the Scriptures, knowing that every verse was written for me and applies to me, and knowing they are that which will equip me to build a Kingdom-driven family — in other words, making God's priorities our family's priorities.

Too many women come to the conclusion that it is not necessary that they delve deeply into the law-word of God — that their husbands should do the "heavy lifting" and then teach them. So they focus on the domestic aspect of managing the household (which is fine and good); but too often that leaves them seeing themselves as nothing more than unpaid tutors, maidservants, and chefs. I'm not advocating for abolishing this aspect of running a household, but I have discovered, over time, that the women who come to me for mentoring are often married to men who are serious students of God's Word and avid readers of Rushdoony's books. Many of these women look at the sheer number of pages of the *Institutes of Biblical Law* and become overwhelmed that they'll never ever be able to get

---

2. ibid., 20.

through it, let alone digest it. Once they understand that by avoiding the study of God's law they are limiting their role as a helper to their husband, they are willing to give it a try. The method I employ as a mentor is tackling a section at a time, letting each woman move at her own pace.

I have taught through the *Institutes* twice (both in person and online) with groups of women across three continents and a number of my previous students are attending this conference in person or online today. Let me assure you, we got through it. I jokingly referred to it as the "dos equis study" which in Spanish means 2 x's because one had to have 2 x chromosomes to attend. Little did I know that at times there were men on the other end of the Skype call quietly listening in.

I am currently engaged in another run-through with a group of women on Tuesday nights. We have just embarked on the chapter dealing with the fourth commandment. This doesn't cover the individual studies I have had or am currently having with various women using Rushdoony's seminal work on the law on a one-on-one basis.

In all cases, what has become apparent to me is that the life of the family and the family culture become much more Christ-centered when both husband and wife have a working knowledge of the law.

God never intended for Adam's helpmeet to be just a pretty ornament. That stereotype is a carry-over from the Enlightenment and cheapens the institution of marriage that God chose to use as analogous to Christ's relationship to the church.

Another stereotype that has made its way into some aspects of Christian culture today is the fallacious standard that women in the course of day-to-day life are to be muted and blindly submissive. As Rushdoony cuttingly states:

> Adam in Eden no doubt had at least one pet dog from the moment of his creation as a mature man . . . If all he needed was someone or something to boss and to order to come at his whistle, or his beck and call, a dog would have been sufficient. But God said, "It is not good that the man should be alone; I will make him a help meet for him" (Gen. 2:18).

A helpmeet is *not* a doormat, but a subordinate and necessary partner.[3]

So the role that the wife/mother carries out in the household is not one of unquestioning obedience to her husband. That is why knowing and understanding the law of God is vital to a healthy marriage. What if her husband is wrong? What if he is sinning? For a woman to render unquestioning obedience to her husband is sin.

Deuteronomy 29:29 states:

> The secret *things belong* unto the Lord our God: but those *things which are* revealed *belong* unto us and to our children for ever, that *we* may do all the words of this law.

Wives and mothers must do all the words of the law and a godly husband should relish his wife's input. All authority is bounded by God's law and it severely diminishes the family if one member of the partnership is silenced and sidelined in important matters. Rushdoony noted that:

> The Puritan wives were not given to servile obedience, and they provided the strong-willed helpmeets necessary to the conquest of a continent. The Puritan men held that the Kingship of Christ was the only absolute power, and they acted on that principle.[4]

Rushdoony goes on to state that any other view is a throwback to pagan antiquity. He concludes,

> [T]he people of God must be taught that it is a *sin* to *require* unquestioning obedience, *and* a *sin* to *yield* it. We are not God: we cannot require or expect for ourselves the absolute obedience due unto God. We are not man's creature: we cannot yield to any man the absolute and unquestioning obedience due only unto God. The church must be cleansed of the requirement of pagan obedience or it will continue under the judgment of God.[5]

---

3. R. J. Rushdoony, *Salvation and Godly Rule* (Vallecito, CA: Ross House Books, [1983] 2004), 495–496.
4. ibid., 498.
5. ibid., 498–499.

A man carrying out his dominion calling in his profession or livelihood needs to count on his wife to handle the affairs of the household while he works in the "city gate." This concept of the city gate has applicability across many institutional and professional lines.

A way to look at this is men disciple the nations while women train up the next generation to work alongside those who are bringing the law and the gospel to every aspect of life and living. I am not referring to stereotypical views of what it means to train up the next generation. While teaching children to read and write and compute is part of the package, it is not, nor will ever be the point of the entire endeavor. The purpose remains to "seek the Kingdom of God and His righteousness." If you fail to equip the women whom God has ordained to keep watch over the next generation as they grow into maturity, then those converted to the faith will not have any good models and paradigms to see how, as new creations in Christ, they must live their lives. Our children are thus integral to discipling the nations.

Men conquer the world for Christ; women work to preserve that which is conquered. But we see a dearth of training for women ready to do this. That is why my emphasis remains on helping women realize and embrace the power-base that resides with a woman educated in God's law, who makes her family the center of her concern, and focuses her teaching on the law of God. This doesn't mean that she has no other concerns, but if her family is relegated to the back burner, important Kingdom work is being shifted from God's first choice (her) to state nannies, paid substitutes, or the ungodly. Someone has to be managing the household. That someone is the kind of woman that unmarried men should be looking for to marry. Married men should be encouraging their wives to model the description of a Kingdom-driven woman laid out in Proverbs 31.

Note that it is King Lemuel's mother whose words are described as prophecy. In other words, she was speaking for God! Let's go through the criteria for a Kingdom-driven wife and mother.

1. She is a virtuous woman whose price is far above precious gems: The Geneva Bible uses the word *pearls*. Other translations use the

words *jewels* or *rubies*. So whether this is referring to the amount of dowry the law prescribes to show good faith on the part of a man in proposing marriage or just detailing that a good wife is extremely valuable — we're told this is something for a man to pursue.

2. Her husband's heart safely trusts in her. How can a godly man trust his wife if she does not know how to live her life lawfully, under God — not making up the rules as she goes along? Can he trust her not to spend more than their income allows? Can she be trusted not to enter into financial agreements that he has not approved? A husband needs to know that his wife "has his back" and that she will stand by him when he has tough decisions to make. The notes in the Geneva Bible add that such a virtuous woman is a check against her husband using unlawful means to make a living.

3. She does him good and not evil all the days of her life. The implication is that she can ascertain the difference between good and evil, and that her actions will be in harmony with the Scriptures. This very much ties in with a husband trusting his wife with their children as she establishes godly standards in their lives.

4. She is a hard worker and is entrepreneurial in her efforts. She is the multitasker that God designed a woman to be. It is no small feat to be able to grow a child inside of you, nurse another, and manage the rest of the children of the household. I know many a woman who manages to do just that. Why wouldn't a man relish such a wife who holds down the fort allowing him to single-mindedly pursue his work of dominion?

5. She is not an emaciated flower consumed and distracted with the world's standard of beauty. She is strong and healthy, both physically and mentally. The skinny supermodel type is the antithesis of a virtuous woman. As the virtuous woman works to maximize the prosperity of her family, she provides good wholesome food for herself and the rest of the crew to maintain her own health and that of those under her charge.

6. She is industrious and is pleased with the work of her hands. She knows the product she is striving for and evaluates herself by God's standards. She can be confident that if she is putting the law

into practice, the unrealistic and shallow standards of the world are not a threat to her nor do they condemn her. She is pleased with progressive sanctification and relies on the guidance of her husband and the Word of God to correct and instruct her.

7. Her care and concern for the poor and needy is tied in with her availability, not only to perceive the needs of others, but (along with her children) to be ready to address those needs. Her volunteerism and instilling that quality in her children makes her a beacon to those who need guidance and assistance.

8. She is providential regarding the physical, emotional, educational, and spiritual needs of those in her care and seeks answers to problems that arise. She is not intimidated by threats from statists or school boards or nosey neighbors for she is not surprised or taken off guard by the attacks of an ungodly culture. She is well-read when it comes to medical issues, learning problems, and matters of health, so that her children are given the time and attention to thrive. Her commitment to her children involves networking with other women to deal with situations not familiar to her.

9. She cares for her own needs as she cares for those under her care. She's not a martyr or a bondservant in her work. Her clothing being "purple" signifies her regard for her God-ordained status and authority. She is the manager of the household, not the household slave. That is why she starts early on to teach her children their place in the family and instructs them in household responsibilities.

10. Because she is competent about decisions that need to be made and doesn't burden him with trivial matters, her husband is known in the gates — in other words free to transform the culture around him. She knows his preferences and is used to discussing family matters with him, heeding his counsel, so she can act in ways that will please him and bring him honor among those in the public square.

11. If, with her skill or training, she can add to the family income, she does so. However she must never neglect her first area of concern — the ways of her household. Even if other family members or friends watch over her children in her absence, she must maintain their well-being as a first priority.

12. She is known for her strength, honor, wisdom, and grace in her actions and her speech. This means that other women seek her out and know that she will counsel them Biblically, not engaging in pity parties or slams against their husbands. Her experience with children will allow her to help younger mothers who may be struggling.

13. She is the household manager, and, rather than shirking work, she pursues it with vigor, all the while being a teacher and example to her children so that in her absence they can manage and care for the demands of running the home.

14. In the end, her biggest fans and supporters are her husband and children because she creates an atmosphere where they can all thrive. Their successes are her successes and she need not seek acclaim outside her family. In the end, she has her priorities in order and receives honor and appreciation from her family, extended family, and brothers and sisters in the Lord. Because she fears God and keeps His commandments as her whole duty, she leaves a legacy to future generations, helping to create the context for dominion.

She truly is the glue that holds the family together, bridging the gap in conflicts and always stressing the need for repentance, reconciliation, and restoration.

Do any of us do this flawlessly? No one that I have met. But these are the criteria that we should make a priority, trusting that God will bring the wisdom needed to correct mistakes and rectify faulty thinking.

If the description sounds challenging, that is because it is. Although redeemed, we still have that tendency to buck against responsibilities. As Rushdoony expressed it, every person born into the world comes embedded with a revolt against maturity — a desire to take the easy way out and shy away from our duties.

He points out,

A central error of humanism and modernism has been the belief in "the natural goodness of man." By its failure to take into account the fact of the fall, humanism has been unable to cope effectively with the problem of sin. It has consistently added to man's predicament by ascribing evil to the environment rather than to the heart of man, and it has been unable to penetrate man's psychology because of its willful blindness.[6]

I hope you see why it is so important for the woman of the house to understand this. If she is going to assist her husband in his dominion work and disciple her children to be people of character and integrity when they reach adulthood, she must not be blinded by the lie that those around her are basically good. She needs to identify and confront sin when she sees it, and with little sinners running around, she will see it.

That is why when I begin a mentoring relationship with women (whether single, married or widowed), I begin with a study of God's law using Rushdoony's *Institutes*. Nothing is more fulfilling for me than seeing their sanctification unfold as they begin to think lawfully and turn the corner from struggling to find the Biblical answers to having a clear method to ferret them out.

Some say that the husband should be the one to teach his wife. I don't disagree. But many men don't. I believe that the best teachers teach their students how to think, rather than what to think, and I am willing to help someone who wishes to learn. I make it a point to let them know that I have no desire to replace their husband, father, or pastor. I explain that in my own life, when I have a question regarding something I don't understand in the Bible, I do what the Scripture says and ask my husband first. We'll discuss it — bringing to bear our understanding of the Word to figure it out. If we end up without a conclusion or disagree on something, he often suggests we seek out people we trust to help elucidate the issue. (Two of those men, Mark Rushdoony and Martin Selbrede, are often whom we go to.) Besides, there are times when a woman's perspective can help another woman sort out problems in the household and I endeavor to be that "Titus 2 woman" showing a woman how to better love her husband and children.

Is it any wonder that the enemies of God want to remove women from the sphere of power and dominion in their homes and divert

6. Rushdoony, *Revolt Against Maturity*, 13.

them from the high calling of being the Woman of the House — the term I like to use for wife and mother?

Please don't get me wrong. If you are currently working outside the home for financial reasons, I'm not saying you should immediately quit. What I am saying is that your responsibilities are not lessened because you have an outside job. You may need to continue in your work, or choose to do so, but your role of wife and mother cannot be a secondary priority. In essence, you will need to work double-time in order to be found faithful before God.

There are so many things that fall to the trustee family to maintain. With families going in all different directions, one such area is the care of the elderly and the sick. Without the woman of the house to oversee this, it falls to paid substitutes and government handouts. One of the great learning experiences of my life was the opportunity and privilege of caring for my husband's mother — my mother-in-law — in the last years of her life. Not only was it the correct thing to do, but it was a living example to my children that this is what families do.

So what is the woman of the house responsible to do?

1. She is to love God with all her heart, soul, and strength.

2. She is to equip herself to be ready to give her children the reason for the hope that is within her by knowing what she believes and why.

3. She is to teach her children that they are God's creatures and therefore subject to His law and she must instruct them in that law.

4. She is to be a model for them in what is lawful and acceptable behavior.

5. She is to help them understand that sin is doing other than what God commands — either by commission or omission.

6. She is to discipline them, not based on arbitrary standards but godly ones, and apply timely correction when they have violated God's commands.

7. She is to teach them how to think in terms of God's law as the means to avoid trouble and problems.

8. She is to provide them with a regular interaction with faithful Christians outside the immediate family in order to have buffers when difficult times arise.

9. She is to trust God to equip her in her weakness — knowing that His grace is sufficient and that His strength is manifest in her weakness.

In closing, I'd like to remind us that building a Kingdom-driven family is not an end unto itself, but the means by which we fulfill the Great Commission and pursue the Kingdom of God. As a result, we need not be fearful of our tomorrows, nor the problems we face today. That very same law that will usher in the Kingdom of God, gives us the assurance that as we providentially work to serve God's Kingdom, the necessities of life will be supplied.

13

Of Course There's Time

Many women claim that they are just too busy to put serious reading into their schedules. By serious reading, I mean books on a variety of subjects that will improve a woman's ability to run her household better. A woman's response to a problem or crisis that arises in her household will be enhanced to the degree she has become competent in a variety of areas prior to the need. With all the resources available in the internet age, she can become knowledgeable in the subject where she needs assistance.

Suppose one of her children is having difficulty in acquiring a skill that older children learned easily. Rather than categorize the child as "slow" or "delayed," the mother needs to do some online research, seek out experienced mothers, and possibly make a trip to the library. These efforts can help the mother understand how to help the child through this learning difficulty.

How about a diagnosis of diabetes that her spouse receives? If she has already been informing herself on health issues, she has many more protocols (including alternative ones) to pursue to help her husband control and possibly reverse the problem. With such a scenario, the doctor becomes just one of a number of resources at the family's disposal.

How about a controversy affecting those in her church family? Knowing the particulars of opposing points of view will help her family maneuver through any hard feelings and potentially facilitate reconciliation. In addition, being firmly grounded in the Word of God is essential for assessing church conflicts, to differentiate between orthodoxy issues and those of hurt feelings.

In all these areas, being out in front of issues is far superior to having to learn on the fly. This acquired knowledge can prove useful to other families going through similar circumstances. Time invested in becoming well-versed in a variety of topics will pay back in future dividends for more than just her own household.

My point is a simple one. The wife/mother (woman of the house) needs to assume the perspective that she is the household manager rather than the laborer of the home. The presence of children actually enhances her ability to learn her craft better. The children can be assigned age-appropriate tasks, thereby giving their mom the opportunity to become a better manager. Since the family members will all benefit from the fruits of her learning, they have a vested interest in giving her time to pursue her ongoing education.

So teach us to number our days, that we may apply our hearts unto wisdom. (Ps. 90:12)

14

Women Working Outside the Home

Periodically the subject of women working outside the home comes up in discussions with women I mentor. The question is: Now that this practice is so entrenched in our culture, is it a practice that honors God or not? The first thing we need to consider is the responsibilities that the Word of God gives to women. Only after this subject is understood can we determine whether a particular activity falls within the jurisdiction God assigns to women.

All the commandments of God have applicability to all people — male and female — although they will be applied, in some cases, differently for each gender. Second, where the Bible directly addresses matters pertaining to women, such as Proverbs 31, special attention needs to be given as to why certain aspects of a woman's character and activities are highlighted. In the case of Proverbs 31, even though the speaker is addressing her son, the chapter establishes the Biblical characteristics of a worthy woman.

When it comes to adjudicating whether or not an activity (not just employment) is suitable and honorable for a woman to pursue outside the home, care must be taken not to resort to an either/ or mentality. Too many people are quick to automatically conclude that anything other than a home-based choice is wrong. This sets up the caricatured perspective that a woman has to abandon any outlet of creativity or fulfillment other than the care of her family. God's way doesn't posit a conflict of interests in a woman's life, but rather a harmony of interests. In order for a woman to stand with a clear conscience before God in the choices she makes, she needs to evaluate the trade-offs involved and determine if God's law-word is being honored in her decision.

A personal story highlights this well. At the time, I was a wife and the mother of two children with my elderly mother-in-law living with us. As a result of some organizing work that I had done well, I was asked to consider a position as campaign manager for a lawyer who was running for city council. To say that I was flattered is an understatement. They explained that I was their top candidate for this position.

I was a homeschooling mom and actively involved in not only educating my children, but running and administering some of their extracurricular activities, not to mention my normal household responsibilities and transporting my mother-in-law to her medical appointments. So, I knew that this undertaking would be a challenge if I hoped to do all these things well. Nonetheless, with my husband's approval, I decided to attend a meeting to discuss the offer further.

I put on my most professional clothes (something I hadn't done for some time) and had a good meeting with the men of the committee. They explained that if the candidate won, I would have the option of running his district office. The men who were trying to convince me knew the buttons to push. They explained that this would be an opportunity for me to exercise dominion and influence local government to be more Biblically oriented. I told them that I would discuss this with my husband and get back to them.

Meanwhile, back at home, I had left my two children with a babysitter as I didn't feel that my mother-in-law (in her late 80s) would be comfortable with them by herself. Whereas I expected that things might not be smooth, I never anticipated the disaster I found when I returned home. The babysitter had gotten on the wrong side of my son, and my daughter was crying hysterically. My mother-in-law was aggravated, and the babysitter made it clear that she would never work for us again. After I drove her back home, I noticed that I was almost out of gas and stopped to fill up my tank. Already frustrated and upset over the mess I returned to, I forgot the gas cap for my car. I only realized it when I got home and, in the short time that it took for me to return to the gas station, it was gone!

By the time my husband returned home from work, I managed to have everyone settled. He and I talked. We both decided that God had spoken through the circumstances of the evening, and we came to the obvious conclusion that, although I was capable to handle the job offered, this was not the right time. The next day, I called and declined the offer.

Pursuing this activity outside the home did not fall into the category of sin, in and of itself. The issue that became obvious was that I wouldn't be able to address my responsibilities at home and do a good job for the candidate. If a similar offer were presented to me today, since my circumstances are radically different (all children schooled and grown), I could consider it.

Whenever a woman takes on responsibilities outside her home, volunteer or paid, she must realize that her role as wife and mother is primary. Too often, a woman who has paid employment elsewhere is under the authority of others who don't have her family's well-being as their top priority. So, for example, if her child is sick, rather than be the person who remains home to care for him, she may shuffle him off to daycare or school, sometimes even masking his symptoms. (Some daycares and schools allow children to attend who have fevers so long as they are not above 102 degrees!) Thus, money and job security end up trumping her role as mother. If she does decide to remain with her ill child, she may be sacrificing a project or potentially compromising her standing at work. In either case, there is a conflict of interests.

We need to remember that the primary "employer" in our lives is the triune God, and we must make His concerns and priorities our concerns and priorities. To do otherwise is to invite His judgment and displeasure. Whereas outside work can provide additional funds, a sense of accomplishment, and, at times, prestige, we must be more concerned with storing up the treasures in heaven that God promises to those who are faithful.

15

Present Yourself Approved

The response to God's gift of salvation should be an overwhelming desire to please God in obedience to His commandments. If this is not present, it is safe to assume that one has not been visited by the Holy Spirit, even though a person may be influenced by the Christian culture around him. But for those who have the Holy Spirit, there exists a drive to establish oneself truly on the path that leads to life.

Educating oneself and one's children in the ways of the Lord must be a primary concern for those who are called by God into His Kingdom service. Not only must they acquire a godly perspective and worldview by adhering to the Scripture, they must also unearth the lies, myths, and deceptions attendant to their past humanistic education. This can be a daunting task, but one that, if not undertaken, leads to the impotency of a shallow faith and inconsequential cultural transformation efforts.

So, how does one present oneself approved to God when the task at hand takes so much time and seems too difficult to attain? Since our sanctification is progressive, we need to develop a godly patience in the pursuit.

R. J. Rushdoony describes it this way:

> Very simply stated, what this means is that, where we have a confident expectation of something, that hope or confidence gives us the patience to wait for it. Thus, even as patience is associated with hope,

so by implication the loss of hope means impatience. When we have no hope, both waiting and tribulations become meaningless to us, and we cannot then patiently endure them . . .

Biblical patience is inseparable from hope; it means a waiting with confidence, that the future holds great reward and an assured fulfillment.[1]

Any steps taken to become versed in the law of God without a prior conviction of victory are likely to have meager results at best, or end up in failure at worst. That is why the foundation of all preparation to learn, live, and teach the commandments of God must include the expectation that the endeavor will be successful. Obedience and victory are two sides of the same coin.

Here is the patience of the saints: here are they that keep the commandments of God, and the faith of Jesus. (Rev. 14:12)

Rushdoony continues,

This patience means that they believe God's law and rest assured that its judgment will fully overwhelm all evil-doers. Patience thus has, *first*, a confidence that this world, being totally God's creation, will see God's victory and the vindication of His people. *Second*, patience means also the certainty that God's total judgment will be meted out to all offenders, who "shall drink of the wine of the wrath of God" (Rev. 14:10).[2]

To divert one's attention away from the task of discipling the nations, because of fearful concerns over the plans of statist politicians or oppressive school boards, implies doubt in the accuracy and veracity of God's Word. When the people of God are on task in Kingdom service, the gates of hell shudder in their imminent defeat, not the other way around.

Acquiring Knowledge

Once the certainty of victory is presupposed, the task at hand is to learn God's perspective on *everything*. This means evaluating all

1. R. J. Rushdoony, *Revolt Against Maturity* (Vallecito, CA: Ross House Books, 1987), 257.
2. ibid., 258.

books and materials studied with the template of God's Word over them all. True knowledge is not a collection of un-interpreted *facts*, as no such thing exists. True knowledge seeks to comprehend the divine purpose in all things. When many claim that the Bible is not sufficient to learn about technology or physics, etc. (e.g., "The Bible isn't a textbook!"),[3] we must whole-heartedly disagree. For there can be no true understanding of any realm if we deny God His preeminence.

Rushdoony again,

> The unbeliever seeks... "knowledge in the abstract"... Abstract knowledge is the attempt to interpret all things without reference to God. God is abstracted from reality, and things are interpreted, not in terms of God, but in terms of themselves...
>
> Nothing has any residue of being or meaning which can be abstracted from God and His creative purpose. Every atom of every particular thing is a creation of God, and it is only truly knowable in terms of Him. To attempt the interpretation of anything without God is to attempt the impossible.[4]

Does this mean that only books and materials from Christian publishers are reliable tools to learn about the past and present world around us? Ideally, the answer would be "yes," but a close look throughout the landscape tells us we aren't there yet when it comes to excellent offerings in all areas.[5] The foundational understanding needs to be in conformity to God's Word, not at odds with it. Thus, knowing and being able to apply the Biblical worldview to one's study of biology or chemistry or physics or nutrition or medicine or law, is the only sure-fire way to come to correct conclusions. We can learn from secular sources providing we use the standard of God's law-word to separate fact from fiction.

---

3. Most textbooks are full of regurgitated humanistic conclusions that are meant to stultify true knowledge; so, in that sense, the Bible is most definitely not a textbook!

4. R. J. Rushdoony, *Revolt Against Maturity*, 23.

5. This is a market wide open to those who understand theonomy and reconstruction and desire to share their knowledge in particular areas.

Research — A Key Tool

Once a person has a good foundational understanding of the law of God and knows how to reference it when the need arises to gain knowledge in a particular area, developing the ability to research additional sources is a vital skill. Research involves more than just learning, it is the application of wisdom, understanding, discretion, and discernment to the subject being pursued.

Webster defines the word "research" as both a noun and a verb:

> **research**, n. Diligent inquiry or examination in seeking facts or principles; laborious or continued search after truth.
> **research**, v.t.
> 1. To search or examine with continued care; to seek diligently for the truth.
> 2. To search again; to examine anew.

When one assumes the role of researcher, the earlier concept of *patience* needs to be in the forefront, for brick-and-mortar libraries or internet searches can result in many contradictory points of view. An honest pursuit of knowledge that is consistent with Scripture will deliver reliable answers (victory) and allow you to plot a course of action (dominion). It should be noted, this is an activity that might take weeks, months, years, or even a lifetime to fully achieve.

Seeking the counsel of Biblically sound Christian experts in the field being investigated is a must, since you will need someone to help you understand underlying concepts you are unfamiliar with.[6] It is vital that in the pursuit of your research, there should be no expectation of good outcomes if you are not constantly evaluating the information you receive up against the Biblical standards. In other words, this is thoroughly tied in to one's spiritual condition and right-standing as one whose primary concern in life is to "fear God and keep His commandments."

---

6. I have made use of our family chiropractor who is an avid student of health, nutrition, exercise, and rehabilitation as my tutor to understand and evaluate various sources of information. I will often schedule a visit for that specific purpose, knowing that it is as important to see him when I am well (so I can stay well), as when I am feeling ill.

Besides being wise, the Preacher also taught the people knowledge, weighing and studying and arranging many proverbs with great care. The Preacher sought to find words of delight, and uprightly he wrote words of truth. The words of the wise are like goads, and like nails firmly fixed are the collected sayings; they are given by one Shepherd. My son, beware of anything beyond these. Of making many books there is no end, and much study is a weariness of the flesh. The end of the matter; all has been heard. Fear God and keep his commandments, for this is the whole duty of man. For God will bring every deed into judgment, with every secret thing, whether good or evil. (Eccles. 12:9–14, ESV)

Rushdoony sums this up ably when he comments,

The restoration of knowledge and learning means therefore that we must "put on the new man, which is renewed in knowledge after the image of him that created him" (Col. 3:10). On no other basis can there be a renaissance of knowledge . . . [G]odly knowledge or wisdom "is a tree of life to them that lay hold upon her" (Prov. 3:18).[7]

Here are some examples.

Health

Suppose you were trying to avert the onset of diabetes, knowing that it is a prevalent malady in your family. Suppose you had been told that you were heading in that direction and therefore needed to follow a particular diet and lifestyle. How would you evaluate the advice given? Would you follow it because the person telling you these things wore a white coat and had a stethoscope around her neck? How would you know if her advice was genuinely researched and not influenced by rewards she would earn if you followed her directives?

Obviously, you would have to have some understanding of how your body works, what causes diabetes, what insulin is, and how your pancreas produces it. Some might say, "Well, that's why I go to the doctor. I didn't go to medical school — she did." But as believers we

---

7. Rushdoony, *Revolt Against Maturity*, 29.

often disagree with what the medical profession routinely upholds regarding abortion, euthanasia, stem cell research, and vaccinations. Unless someone has a working knowledge of subjects filtered through the lens of Scripture, they are doomed to be blown around (Eph. 4:14) by any humanistic doctrine they may be fed.

Extracurricular Instruction for Children

When parents desire that their children learn a musical instrument or develop proficiency in a particular sport, they look for an instructor. Especially if the parents are venturing into territory unfamiliar to them, there has to be some standard by which they make their selection. Certainly finances and location will factor into it, but most importantly there should be a sense of how any given teacher will present the material to be learned to the children.

Once again, the lens or template of Scripture needs to be applied. The many things to consider and evaluate include: character of the instructor, expertise, and will parents be allowed to sit in on the instruction, etc. None of these things will be apparent in an ad in the yellow pages or on craigslist. Even word-of-mouth is only reliable if you are certain that you share the same world and life view of those making recommendations.

Pursuing Higher Education

When the time comes for young people to begin to plot the course for their future, many decisions need to be made. It is important that decisions are informed by Biblical principles, including all the implications of the career path according to what God is calling them to do.[8] Once they establish a sense of what they wish to focus

---

8. When I taught writing to my own children as well as those who were in co-op classes or privately tutored by me, I always assigned early on an essay entitled "What is God Calling Me to Do," requiring that they explained based on their talents and inclinations an area they thought they might wish to pursue. A major focus was finding out the necessary prerequisites along with interviewing someone who was already working in that capacity. This is a needed step before one can actually research the best way to pursue higher education.

on, research needs to be done to make wise choices in school selection, day or online classes, full or part time, etc.

Parents should partner with their children in this endeavor because the ramifications of the decision made will affect the entire family. Seeking out those who have gone to a particular school, and asking them what things they would do differently, can help in preventing wasted classes or, worse yet, antagonistic professors. Being able to differentiate your own situation from theirs allows you to accept or reject ideas in a positive way. For this reason, parents need to be years ahead of when decisions will need to be made so that the student is not forced into negative situations.

Presenting Oneself Approved

Not all things are known in factual detail by the believer, but he has the principle and the sight by which all things are seen or perceived. His ability to see or know is there; for those who attempt to know on the tempter's terms (Gen. 3:5), there is only blindness.[9]

As we rightly handle the word of truth over all aspects of our lives, and teach others to do so, we are merely giving back to God an increase from the talents He gave to us (Matt. 25:14–30). When we search out matters to understand the context of and calling for our Kingdom service, we can present ourselves approved unto the Lord, not ashamed of our efforts or results.

Do your best to present yourself to God as one approved, a worker who has no need to be ashamed, rightly handling the word of truth. (2 Tim. 2:15, ESV)

---

9. Rushdoony, *Revolt Against Maturity*, 29.

16

Beyond Adequate

Many mothers will admit to feelings of inadequacy when it comes to their calling as a homeschooling parent. Some never went beyond high school, while others didn't go to high school at all. Thus, they feel undereducated for the task of homeschooling their children. Should this lack of "formal" training disqualify them from the undertaking? Should other arrangements be found for the children? Should someone who is "adequate" be sought out for the education of the children?

On the other hand, many women with a college education would rather pursue a career outside the home and leave the care and schooling of their children to others. Many in this group also feel inadequate to handle being a stay-at-home mom with the added responsibility to educate their flock.

There is a well-known expression: *where there is a will, there is a way*. The problem with either group is not a lack of capability or adequacy. After all, if you can read, you can teach someone to read. If you can add, you can teach someone to add. It doesn't require advanced degrees to give a child the tools of learning. What it *does* take is the conviction that it is a mom's responsibility to provide these things — that, in fact, she is the one person best qualified for the task. Why? Because, in the process of teaching a child the mother is given a window into the child's soul. While doing these basic activities a mother has a first-hand view of what makes her child tick.

Does he get frustrated with difficulty, or does he love a challenge? Does she need to do everything she puts her hand to perfectly, or does she enjoy the process as much as the product? These are insights that a mother who is the primary caregiver for her children learns intuitively, because she interacts with them day-in and day-out. This hands-on involvement provides her with useful knowledge, since she knows their personalities well, challenging them where they excel and encouraging them where they struggle.

Women have been fed a diet of myths that encourages them to seek fulfillment outside of family life. That is why the term "house-wife" ends up being an insult in some circles, rather than a status to be honored. It's time for the moms of our culture to own up to the reality that the decayed culture we find ourselves in stems from what has failed to take place in the majority of families for a number of generations. If we don't like what we see, we must change the status quo. How do we change the status quo? By replacing the idea of attaining personal "fulfillment" to one of focusing our attention on building Kingdom-driven families.

Stop giving your best to a company or organization that can replace you in a heartbeat. Instead, make it a priority to *look well to the ways of your household*, knowing that your efforts will be realized in a better future for yourself (yes, you'll be old someday), your family, and the community around you.

Ladies, we need to move from *inadequacy* to *beyond adequacy*. We need to focus our attention on our first priority and then study and learn to prove ourselves up for the task. It's not as difficult as you may have been led to believe. If you have the *will*, there is a *way*!

17

Cultivation

My adult son and I like to exchange audio books with each other. Each of us spends a lot of time driving and these are good ways to redeem that time. Lately I have been listening to one he shared about George Washington. My son knows more about Washington than most people, having made him the subject of much study. I can honestly say that I learned more about our first president from this son whom I homeschooled, than I knew while I was teaching him.

I did not give my son a love of history. God gets the credit for giving him a good mind and the motivation to pursue his interest. My son gets the credit for using the gifts he was given. What I can take credit for is creating an environment for learning and encouraging him, and my other children, to read more than just one book on any given subject. I also emphasized the importance of consulting primary source material in addition to biographies and historical accounts written much later than actual events. I also made it clear that, as a result, they would be in a better position to come to their own conclusions rather than just parrot mine. In truth, when they pursued their interests, they often surpassed my knowledge in various areas.

My fifteen-year-old daughter and I were at the movies watching a film that dramatized a WWII spy mission to capture a German enigma-decoding machine. Much of what was happening went over my head and I muttered, "I don't understand!" She quickly explained what had confused me. How did she know all about submarines when as her teacher I had not made this a focus of study? Later, she explained that on trips to the library she had read a number of books on the subject and that she and her dad had watched a documentary about submarines.

Many home educators consider teaching a daunting task because they do not have time to learn or master all the subjects their children should know. The truth is that they don't have to. By creating a context for learning, establishing a solid foundation in reading, and providing access to information, the whole world is open to students. Especially today with the internet as a research tool, the focus of the home educator should be to instill a Biblical worldview as the way to interpret all that is learned. Building or having access to a library of reliable, challenging material will open the world to your students.

Noted theologian and historian, R. J. Rushdoony, describes in his poem, *The Luxury of Words,* the bounty available to those who are given these tools:

> *The luxury of words, beyond all*
> *Empires, makes me lord*
> *And king. No beggar here,*
> *In majesty, I can afford*
> *The treasured wealth of ages.*
> *Come, gather round and never fear*
> *A drought of gold and silver.*
> *This is the sphere*
> *Of endless plenty, a dower*
> *Of wealth and hammered power.*
> *All words when servant to the Word*
> *Are potentates whose laws are heard.*

The home educating parent is a cultivator of learning, working the soil so that students acquire the necessary framework with which to take dominion in Jesus' name. The payoff is that you will have plenty to learn from them!

18

Underlying Themes

I recently watched two films dealing with Alzheimer's disease and how it affects those diagnosed and their families. While each movie did a good job of showing the challenges and burdens experienced when a family member is afflicted, they also presented worldviews, complete with presuppositions, subtly woven into these personal stories.

One film depicted a committed, elderly man intent on making his wife's final years comfortable as her illness progressed. Being an independent sort, he determined to build a new, single-story home for her on his property to reduce the incidents of falls. This resulted in a conflict with the local bureaucracy regarding what he could and could not do with his land, burdening him with permits and regulations that would seriously hinder his plan. Therefore, along with the surface story, the message of the loss of liberties and the freedom to decide how one uses possessions was an underlying theme. At the film's conclusion, the audience witnessed not only the care and patience of a faithful spouse, but also the extent to which civil government has encroached into our lives.

The second film depicted an accomplished professor who mourns the loss of her intellect and her academic career as she comes to terms with the reality that she has Alzheimer's disease. The story unfolds in a patient manner, causing the audience to feel what this woman feels as she confronts a grim future.

Underlying thematic elements were presented as "givens" rather than ones that merit important moral deliberation. For example, when the family discovers that the Alzheimer's is genetic, the eldest daughter receives testing which confirms she is a carrier. She and her husband, already in the process of fertility treatments, have the embryos tested to ensure that only ones without the genetic defect are implanted. No one raises moral or ethical dilemmas and asks important questions such as what will happen to the other embryos, and are they people or merely blobs of tissue? For them, they have averted a crisis and have made the sensible choice. Since the characters are likable and appear to have no problem with this decision, we, the audience, should accept this as good, standard practice.

The film also conveyed the message that those with Alzheimer's become somewhat less than full people. As the professor experiences the rapid decline in her ability to recall the simplest things, she visits a care facility for Alzheimer's patients to see what her life will be like. She does not like what she sees. As the thought of having such a shallow existence grieves her, she purposes to end her own life. Knowing that she may not remember how to commit suicide, she makes a video to herself, leaving specific instructions: where to find the pills with which to overdose, and when to seize the opportunity to do so. She sees this as a viable alternative that will spare her family the burden of dealing with her as her disease progresses. The movie presents the crisis, but offers nothing other than personal, man-centered solutions.

Most movies (and literature for that matter) present a surface story along with deeper, less obvious, themes woven into the main plot. Unless we come to such encounters with a Biblical worldview, we may be swayed into accepting counterfeit solutions that seem to be compassionate and caring.

The Bible provides us with laws that, as creatures of the Almighty, we must embrace fully, whether or not they sit well with us. God's rules are not incidental nor arbitrary. Thus, if a child is born with a handicap or illness, we should not deem this a mistake, but rather an opportunity for service as unto the Lord. If a loved one or we suffer a debilitating injury or illness, rather than focus on how difficult it will be for us or for them, we should embrace it as part of God's sovereign plan and carry on in faith.

We must make the law of God the fabric of our lives. For if we refuse to live by every word that proceeds from the mouth of God, we have become practical secularists. This is what our modern culture wishes us to become, and surrounds us with moving stories to help achieve this result. The goal of God's Kingdom is the total holiness of all things. When we make this our starting and ending points, we will be better able to see the false solutions presented by a culture at war with God.

19

Alloyed Loyalties

"Every time you hear a lie, and every time you hear the truth, you yourself are tested. Is it the lie or the truth which commands your attention?" — R. J. Rushdoony[1]

When you fail to make the Bible the starting point of thought, you end up constructing a worldview built on a faulty foundation. Couple that with man's sinful nature and the wiles of the devil, and you have a recipe for a cultural malignancy that chokes the life out of people. When the Bible is not the focal point of life and the basis for instruction and behavior, the curses outlined in Deuteronomy 28:15–68 result.[2]

There was a time in our nation's history when the Bible was the presuppositional foundation of culture, even if was not consistently followed. The Bible served to create a context of life, because it was recognized as the *text* of life. Webster's 1828 *Dictionary* reflects this fact.

> **text**, *noun* [Latin *textus*, woven.]
>
> 1. A discourse or composition on which a note or commentary is written. Thus we speak of the *text* or original of the Scripture, in

---

1. R. J. Rushdoony, *A Word in Season*, vol. 1 (Vallecito, CA: Ross House Books, 2010), 56.
2. U.S. presidents used to take their oath of office with their hand on the Bible opened to Deuteronomy 28 acknowledging that their actions would bring God's blessings for obedience and His cursings for disobedience.

relation to the comments upon it. Infinite pains have been taken to ascertain and establish the genuine original *text*

2. A verse or passage of Scripture which a preacher selects as the subject of a discourse.

3. Any particular passage of Scripture, used as an authority in argument for proof of a doctrine. In modern sermons, texts of Scripture are not as frequently cited as they were formerly.

4. In ancient law authors, the four Gospels, by way of eminence.

Phrases such as, "do onto others," and "follow the Golden Rule," were part of the vernacular because Jesus Christ had yet to be systematically removed from the public square. While faithfulness to the Word of God was not practiced flawlessly, it was most often preached, sometimes fervently, sometimes nominally.

Today we face a different situation. Because many pastors strive not to offend their congregations or visitors, many who profess belief in Christ merely know somethings about the Bible rather than having made it a priority to understand it and its implications. They fail to comprehend it and refuse to embrace it as the command word from God given as the instruction for holiness in day-to-day living. Biblical literacy is at such a low point that erroneous phrases that have no root in Scripture have become entrenched in "Christian talk." To name a few: "Hate the sin; love the sinner," "We are not under law but under grace," "Isn't it good that God is patient with us even though we fail to obey?" "I can always repent right before I die," "God's Word says not to judge," God will never give me more than I can handle," etc.[3]

These are not gleaned from the text of Scripture. They fall into the category of pretexts and end up being justifications for not following God's law-word. God's gift of the Scriptures is for the express purpose of communicating His intent for mankind. Thus, any deviation from the Creator's blueprint amounts to a pretext, as man determines for himself what is right and what is not (Gen. 3:5). Webster's definition is to the point,

---

3. These "Christian talk" expressions amount to perversions of Scripture to satisfy a humanistic framework.

pretext, *noun* [Latin *proetextus.*] Pretense; false appearance; ostensible reason or motive assigned or assumed as a color or cover for the real reason or motive.

Fallen man is full of pretextual living. The first chapter of Romans clearly delineates that this is not due to ignorance, but rather the suppression of the truth in unrighteousness (Rom. 1:18).

When the church, entrusted with preaching the full counsel of God, and families, commissioned to raise and educate their children in the nurture and admonition of the Lord, fail to exercise their God-ordained duties within their God-ordained jurisdictions, generations grow up without the necessary framework from which to order and conduct their lives. When the commandments of God are not taught and internalized, relativism rules the day and faulty presuppositions become the basis for life and action. When God's watchmen neglect their duties, the walls are easily scaled, and lies replace truth.

Deuteronomy 11:19 specifies the comprehensive manner with which the commandments of God are to be taught:

> You shall teach them to your children, talking of them when you are sitting in your house, and when you are walking by the way, and when you lie down, and when you rise.

The Bible does more than present God's commandments and statutes; it contains detailed stories that demonstrate the positive consequences of faithful living and the negative penalties for disobedience. The Bible must be the text from which standards of right and wrong are established, thereby creating a context in which we are to live and move and have our being (Acts 17:28).

Half Truth — Whole Lie

We have moved past the token Christianity of the last century, and now with the ridicule and caricature of things Christian, we are presented stories where the context of life within the Biblical framework is never considered. What does the context of life look like when the Word of God and the law of God are absent from a culture's literature, film, and music, and professing believers continue to consume counterfeits? The result is a form of religion without the power thereof (2 Tim. 3:5).

Many Christian parents judge modern media based on the rating scale of G, PG, PG-13, R, and X. Because an orthodox Christian worldview is absent among most churchgoers, foul language, nudity, and sexual innuendo end up being the only disqualifiers for what is acceptable for Christians and their children to view.[4] Rarely do Christians examine the storyline, characters, and underlying ethics of a story on the basis of God's law-word.

Some of the biggest box-office successes for both children and adults, while they may not contain abusive language or immodesty, suffer fatally because they eliminate the premise that man's chief end is to glorify God and worship Him alone. In fact, God is completely absent from the lives of the characters, who sin without negative consequences and manage quite well without a fear of the Lord. In other words, these films dish out lies, and if some aspect of truth is communicated, it is not attributed to Jesus Christ as the source of truth. Even well-meaning attempts at depicting Christianity favorably are hindered because they do not do so straightforwardly.[5] The net result is that the consumers of such media end up being double-minded in their orientation to life and their responsibilities to the Kingdom of God. R. J. Rushdoony notes,

> To be "double minded" (or, literally, two-souled, or two-minded) means to be "unstable in all (our) ways" (James 1:8); it means an inability to function, and it prevents us from receiving anything from the Lord (James 1:7). The double-minded man is one who halts between two opinions, who wants the advantages of both but the liabilities of neither. The problem with the double-minded is not that he has two substances, mind and body, making up his being, but that he is unwilling

---

4. How many actually live by this diminished standard is questionable.

5. There are some notable exceptions from brothers Alex and Stephen Kendrick. Their films *Flywheel, Facing the Giants, Fireproof, Courageous,* and *War Room* have storylines that are deliberately Christian. Their main characters are unashamedly followers of Jesus Christ, and the films demonstrate the consequences of sin.

to commit himself openly to either one or the other of two moral decisions. He wants sin without the consequences of sin, and virtue without the responsibilities of virtue. Double-mindedness is a moral, not a metaphysical, fact.[6]

Some justify their consumption of modern media as a harmless diversion during one's leisure time. They argue that they are able to separate the wheat from the chaff—the good from the bad in film, music and television. More often than not, this is a pretext for failing to submit the totality of their life (including their off time) to the Word of God. Indeed, the very concept of leisure itself is not Biblical in its orientation. As Rushdoony points out, leisure is not the same as rest.

> Leisure is thus an attempt to escape from God's world of law and grace. It is an attempt to ground man in his supposed autonomy. Leisure activity becomes more and more imaginative in its lawlessness, and man seeks to build his Great Community around the principle of man's freedom from the Kingdom of Necessity, i.e., from God's world of law. Man's dream of rest is thus total leisure, totally free and autonomous activity outside of God, with a world of slave-machinery doing all the work. Perfect automation and perfect leisure is the goal.[7]

By allowing those at war with God to provide the entertainment and diversions of life (be they sports, music, film, or television), believers are participating in their own enslavement. The seeds sown in their thinking transfer into their speech (learning to be silent about their beliefs in the public square), and eventually they are all too willing to blindly obey despotic, statist mandates in areas such as health, education, and commerce. Would statist overreaches such as mandated vaccinations, enforced health insurance coverage, and the coercion of business owners to violate their consciences be possible if the populace had not been groomed with heavy doses of relativistic humanism? As a culture, our consumption of relativism and

---

6. R. J. Rushdoony, *Institutes of Biblical Law*, vol.2 (Vallecito, CA: Ross House Books, [1982] 2001), 485.

7. ibid., 556.

our rejection of the absolutes of Scripture have left us vulnerable to tyranny and content with living in a world of escape and unreality. Rushdoony points out,

> As a culture declines, it begins to lose its sense of reality and begins to seek refuge in various forms of escapism. This era of humanism is no exception. By its very dedication to modernity, to the present moment, it abandons a long-range view and that historical perspective which is so essential to balance. The self-absorption that marks a decaying culture is especially in evidence today. Metaphysics, the worldview, has given way to psychology, the inner view. As a discipline, metaphysics is in disrepute; as a faith, psychology has conquered even the pulpit, once the stronghold of theology and the cosmic view.
>
> The roots of this change are in modern philosophy... [T]he starting point of philosophy [is] the ostensibly autonomous mind of man... a new center to the universe.[8]

Replacement Stories

There was a time when the stories most were familiar with during their growing up years included names like: Adam and Eve, Noah, David and Goliath, Jonah, and Matthew, Mark, Luke, and John. In addition, the blasphemous practice of using the name Jesus Christ in vain was heavily frowned upon. Today, even youngsters from Christian families know more about Captain America, Batman, Superman, Spiderman, Wolverine, and other superheroes, than they know about their forebears in the faith. Moreover, the disrespect that starts with the abuse of the Lord's name, (so prevalent in all forms of media), filters down to disrespecting parents and other godly authorities. When the Creator of the universe is disregarded, it is any wonder that His earthly representatives are as well?

Biblical law demands specific penalties for certain behaviors. Murder, fornications (including adultery, incest, and homosexuality), kidnapping, theft, slander, etc., all have clearly prescribed penalties. A godly society will deal with these offenses against God and man by

---

8. R. J. Rushdoony, *Noble Savages* (Vallecito, CA: Ross House Books, 2005), 93.

applying the law faithfully. In a humanistic, relativistic society, more attention is given to a law-breaker's motives and environmental circumstances to justify overriding God's law. God's law is then put on trial and pronounced guilty!

The problem with a heavy dose of humanistic entertainment, when viewed uncritically, is that the viewer ends up thinking humanistically rather than Biblically. Consider some of your favorite movies or television programs and assess whether or not God's law is the basis for how people deal with each other or how justice is administered. When all that is posited is another law and another god, the resultant pretexts replace God's text with ungodly alternatives. It, in essence, becomes a negation of God.

> The negation of God means that because hell and justice are denied their ultimacy, then law too is denigrated. Law ceases to represent God's law order and becomes simply the arbitrary will of the State. The State as a law institution gives way to the state as a bureaucracy that sets its own rules and bends men to them.[9]

Humanistic media saturation coupled with statist education, breeds a culture of ostensibly Christian people who think, speak, and behave contrary to their profession of faith. The steady dose of lies (no God, no law) inevitably places them in the enemy camp, despite how saved they may consider themselves. They have missed the call to holiness and their fruits mark them as reprobates.

> In Revelation 22:15, we are told that those outside God's eternal Kingdom, those who are denied access to the tree of life, are "whosoever loveth and maketh a lie." A preference for the lie is a mark of reprobation and of it at the very least a strong disposition to evil.
>
> Scripture, however, summons us to see things differently and to be different. "Ye that love the LORD, hate evil" (Ps. 97:10) . . .
>
> Every time you hear a lie, and every time you hear the truth, you yourself are tested. Is it the lie or the truth which commands your attention?[10]

---

9. R. J. Rushdoony, *To Be As God* (Vallecito, CA: Ross House Books, 2003), 210.

10. R. J. Rushdoony, *A Word in Season*, vol. 1 (Vallecito, CA: Ross House Books, 2010), 56.

Philippians 4:8–9 gives us both a command and a promise. If we focus on what is true, noble, right, pure, lovely, admirable, excellent, and praiseworthy, we can expect God's peace. This is the path to undivided loyalty and cultural victory.

20

The Kingdom-Driven Library

Among the fondest memories of my childhood were our Saturday morning trips to the public library. I loved being around all those books stacked on beautiful shelves nested in mahogany-paneled walls. So it was not really surprising that, early on in my homeschooling career, we made frequent trips to the library and I would allow the children to pick out books on subjects that interested them. However, the more I became a student of R. J. Rushdoony, the more I realized that the public library was by no means a "neutral" place. In fact, I discovered that it was a repository of humanistic views diametrically opposed to a true Christian world and life view, cloaked in an illusion of "neutrality."

One of the key myths of humanism is the idea of neutrality. It is held that the mind of man can be neutral with regard to facts and ideas, and that the scientific method is the way of neutrality. Man can, we are told, calmly and objectively approach and analyze facts and arrive at the truth.

Such a view presupposes neutrality *in the knower* and *the known*. With respect to the knower, man, it assumes that man is not a fallen creature, at war with his Maker. Rather, man is held to be a being capable of approaching factuality objectively and impartially, so that the basic judgments about the nature of things depend upon the mind of man.[1]

---

1. R. J. Rushdoony, *The Philosophy of the Christian Curriculum* (Vallecito, CA: Ross House Books, [1981] 2001), 165.

Upon closer examination, I realized that I needed to peruse a book in its entirety before I would allow my children to exercise their lending privileges. I would need to ascertain if the material was worth reading at all, and, additionally, would it serve my overall purpose in homeschooling—furthering the Kingdom of God? This didn't mean I would automatically disqualify any non-Christian books from being borrowed. However, the value of a particular book (fiction or non-fiction) would be based on whether it would be useful for discussion and instruction.

For example, the library is full of books about nature: rock formations, marine animals, natural wonders, the insect world, and the multitudinous number of plants on our planet. While it is true these books often include beautiful photos, in almost all cases, without fail, each book contains bald-faced lies. Any book that does not credit the Creator of the universe for His handiwork, let alone attributes it to random chaotic processes, is the conveyor of an enormous deception, regardless of how well it is put together. In some cases, I would use these books to teach my children the fallacies of evolution and *Mother Nature*, instructing them about presuppositional thinking as I did.

Again Rushdoony was helpful in my coming to terms with this:

Man . . . is fallen in all his being; he is totally at war with God. Fallen man may manifest no hostility to God, but his indifference is equally an act of war, because he has ruled out God from all consideration in all things. He has in effect declared that God is dead for him, and therefore need not even be considered or thought about. (If my children act as though I do not exist, nor am to be thought about, spoken about or referred to, then they, without a word said, are manifesting hatred of me, and are warring against me.) Man is never neutral with respect to God, nor to anything that is of God. There is no neutrality in man.[2]

Never Say Never

The need to build up our family library became obvious to me during one of our visits to the local library. We had been listening to

---

2. ibid.

a series of lectures on American history and the speaker referenced Blackstone's *Commentaries* (actually *Commentaries on the Laws of England* by Sir William Blackstone) as often quoted by those in early America. I thought it would be a great exercise for my son to see what was contained in them.

When we could not find the entry in the catalogue of books in a neighborhood library, I suggested my son ask the librarian if these books might be in the reference section — able to be read but not borrowed. She agreed to look. She came back after about twenty minutes apologizing that it had taken her so long. She put a book on the table and explained the delay was due to the fact that the book was in the children's section. We were presented with a small paperback book entitled *Blackstone's Magic Tricks for Children*! It would have been funny if it were not so tragic. She truly had no idea what we were asking for.

The last thing I ever imagined myself doing when I was in school was to become a librarian. My reasoning was due to the fact that I had a stereotypical idea of a quiet person sitting behind a desk admonishing noisy folks to "shhh," only to be trapped into running errands for patrons to locate a book that they could not find. Little did I know that a librarian's role includes choosing which books should be in the library, having a very powerful position indeed. Despite my faulty predictions for my future, I became a librarian for my family and for our ministry.

Extending Our Reach

Over my twenty-eight years of active homeschooling, as I bought materials for my family, I realized that I was building a library that could have greater usefulness than just for us. It seemed wasteful not to share my collection after one of my children had used the material and it would be years before the next one needed it. It seemed wasteful to have it just sitting on the shelf. So I made a point of lending out certain curriculum materials to other homeschooling families who couldn't afford their own. This arrangement allowed them to use the materials for the entire school year, or, alternately, as a way to peruse a book or curriculum to see if it was something they wanted to purchase and, if so, they could use my copy until theirs arrived. I also began a collection of historical novels that were a huge hit with my children. Since reading was something that they loved, it became my mission to supply their appetites. Anytime I'd hear of someone "stalled" with their children in their homeschooling pursuits, I could highly recommend some of the fiction we had as a way to revitalize their interest.

To build this library, I spent a considerable amount of money at conferences at the book table. I would often go to such places with book-buying as my major interest. Additionally, if I saw something advertised in a magazine or catalog that looked interesting, I would immediately order it, not being certain it ever would be advertised again. While a portion of my selections would include primary source materials, I kept an eye out for subjects that interested me in fulfilling my role as wife, mother, and home educator. After all, can anyone have too much knowledge?

Your Library Says a Lot about You

When I visit people, I often peruse the books they have on their shelves. It tells you a lot about their world and life view. I imagine I get the same treatment when others visit me. Although I've passed along many of the homeschooling materials I used when actively teaching, I still have quite an assortment of books on a variety of subjects: health, history, theology, music, art, biographies, novels, survival guides, VHS lectures, DVDs, most versions of the Bible, sports, exercise, anatomy, languages, catechisms, how to books, counseling, physics, architecture, marriage, the Constitution, Christian Reconstruction, philosophy, economics, the Federal Reserve, and more.[3]

---

3. I once tried to computerize my library attempting to make a record of all my books. I planned to place them on the shelves according to subject matter. But after a major earthquake my husband insisted that paperbacks get placed on top shelves while bigger books remain on the lower ones. Such ended my ambitious project. I keep track of books "on the shelves" when I go looking for a book I want to reference. It does take time, but the process reminds me of what my library contains.

Have I read all the books that fit on my many bookshelves? No. Have I looked through and read parts of most? Yes. Do I have favorites that I read over and over? Most certainly. And I am most delighted when during a conversation, a topic arises and I can recommend a book from my library.

I have a propensity for buying good material in all forms: hardbacks, paperbacks, Kindle books, etc. But I must admit that, while the digital format is convenient on so many levels,[4] I like the feel of a book and the sense of accomplishment when I finish the last page and place it back on the shelf. One can easily share a book with another, something that is impractical when it is housed on your personal device.

Building a Lending Library

Over the years I have used a wide variety of curricula and audio/video resources to help me in the home education of my children. Some of these were used by all three children; others were acquired to suit the particular needs of one's individual learning style. In the process, I was building quite a good library and a body of knowledge of the various publishers. Then, I began to purchase resources (both new and used) that I felt would be helpful to me to further educate myself to be the best teacher possible for my kids. In time, I needed more and more bookcases to house what would become useful tools for my own children, those I tutored or taught, and eventually to become part of my homeschool lending library. This has been a great outreach for my family as we're always lending out materials for review or a year's worth of use to new homeschoolers and veterans alike.

I suggest that homeschool co-ops and churches make a concerted effort to grow similar libraries in their own cities and communities. With the increasing number of families making the choice to provide a distinctively Christian education to their children, being ready to help is a very pro-active endeavor. By way of example here are some

---

4. There's nothing quite like being able to carry an entire library on one device. For long plane flights, waiting at an appointment, or jury duty with long down times, I find I have a variety of reading options so rewarding, it almost feels like I'm cheating!

general guidelines included in our library agreement:

- There is no fee to borrow materials. However, library materials undergo normal wear and tear, so we encourage donations to help us replace worn-out materials and to expand the library.
- Lending period is for two weeks (unless special arrangements are made).
- Books and other materials are to be returned in the condition they are received.
- In the event library materials are not returned in useable condition, we require that the borrower pay replacement costs in addition to a service fee of $10.
- Any problem with library materials should be brought to our attention immediately.
- Materials are lent to you and your family and should not be lent to other individuals or families. If other families wish to borrow materials, they need to fill out an agreement in order to borrow directly from us.
- It is the responsibility of the borrower to return library materials as agreed and not the responsibility of the library to call and pick them up. However, convenient arrangements can be made for pickup and delivery.
- Lending privileges may be revoked at the discretion of the library staff.
- Since we are now expanding the lending privileges, other conditions may be added to this agreement as experience dictates. In that case, you will be notified in writing of such changes, if and when they occur.[5]

Preparing for the Future

Young people need to build a library of books that they will continue to refer to and have on hand as they mature and begin their own families. Books that have meant a lot to them but belong to their parents' library should be noted and acquired, either through

---

5. This section is taken from an essay that appeared in my second book, *The Homeschool Life* (Vallecito, CA: Chalcedon/Ross House Books, 2008), 113–114.

purchase or entered on a "wish list" for family and friends for birthdays, etc. As C. S. Lewis noted, "No book is really worth reading at the age of ten which is not equally — and often far more — worth reading at the age of fifty and beyond."[6]

I make a point of giving books as presents to graduates. My top choice is R. J. Rushdoony's *Institutes of Biblical Law*. I've often commented that if for some reason I was told we were going to a deserted island and I could only take three books with me, *Institutes*, along with a Bible and a survival guide would make the cut. I usually let the gift recipient know why I've selected this volume. While I have given books as presents over the years, I prefer to lend books. That way, I can find out if the person actually reads it. Give a book as a gift, and it seems pushy to keep inquiring if it has been read. But, lend one out, and your inquiries and reminders are built-in ways of seeing if the book is available for the next person. I have found that the time limit on borrowing helps get the material read!

Chalcedon's Digital Library

R. J. Rushdoony left a legacy of books, essays, journal articles, and lectures. Chalcedon sells many of them and has as one of its primary missions keeping his materials in print. Thus, there is little excuse for people not to have a good collection for their libraries. However, a number of years ago Chalcedon went one step further. By offering the entire Rushdoony collection accessible online at no charge, we made it possible for his profound insights to be shared with anyone with computer access. There are even some individuals who have categorized and organized the collection, making retrieval easy.[7] Thus, there is no excuse for willing students of God's Word not to make use of this resource.

Truth as embodied in the Lord Jesus Christ is what the focus of education should be all about. A library functions as a preserver of that truth by being a repository of information and learning that is

---

6. www.cslewisquotes.webs.com
7. www.pocketcollege.com/index.htm

deemed of value to us in our calling to serve God's Kingdom. Sometimes the information is of the "how to" variety. At other times, materials contained in a library might fall into the "learn what *not* to do" category, demonstrating the deleterious effects of doing so. Without a reliable and available library of information, we are at the deficit of only operating on those thoughts and ideas that are easily accessible and retrievable in our minds. Having a useful library gives us the tools to act in obedience to the Great Commission. But it must be self-consciously built to provide its users with the tools necessary for dominion. It must be founded in the truth of God's Word.

> Truth is never abstract, nor is it some vague idea floating in the heavens. Truth is always relative to whatever is ultimate in our faith. If matter is ultimate for us, then truth is relative to matter, if mind, to mind. If man is ultimate, then truth is contingent and relative to man. For us however, all things having been created by the sovereign and triune God, are relative to Him and to His word. Because the Lord is the ultimate and sovereign Creator, He is therefore the truth in all its fullness, and all else is true in terms of its relation to Him. The more we understand the relation of the physical world in relation to God and His order and purpose in creation, the more we know the truth about creation . . .
>
> Humanistic philosophies of education, and the state schools, are expressions of a religious faith, faith in man . . . Ours is another faith, and we must stand in terms of it, consistently and faithfully.[8]

Substitute the word "library" for "state schools" and Rushdoony is making the case for a Kingdom-driven library!

---

8. Rushdoony, *The Philosophy of the Christian Curriculum*, 168.

21

Stewardship, Not Ownership

I well remember the first moments of holding my son in my arms after he was born. It was the perfect intersection of terror and ultimate joy. Within my arms lay a child who, while no longer dependent upon me for oxygen, still would require my constant care when it came to feeding, clothing, and sheltering him. Firstborns have a greater challenge in life, because they have rookie parents who are thrust into the roles of mother and father, learning as they go. Additionally, for those born to yet to be converted parents, they sometimes have the added hurdle of living through some significant worldview alterations of those who are in authority over them.

My son was just over three years old when I came to faith in Jesus Christ. My husband's conversion was about four months after mine. It wasn't until years later, after my second child was born, that we had a major worldview shift. We went from looking to the Scripture as a series of guidelines that would "help" us approach life to embracing the concept that learning and applying God's law was the way believers in Christ demonstrated their faith. As a result, our family orientation shifted from what we thought was best to what God required of us.

Homeschooling was a natural outworking of this new found perspective and we took our responsibilities in the education of our children seriously. We understood that the buck stopped with us and that we would answer to God for the stewardship of the children He entrusted to our care. However, it was all too easy to step outside the bounds of stewardship and cross over into the realm of ownership. Over the years, as my three children grew, these concepts were tested over and over again.

Young children need guidance and boundaries. Thus, we don't ask their permission to apply the law of God to our family and to their behavior. It is the duty of parents to establish God's standards and to communicate to their children that we, like them, are under the authority of God and thus, subject to blessings for obedience and cursings for disobedience. The evidence of such upbringing is readily apparent to those outside the family. While they may consider such parenting "old-fashioned," there is little dispute that children raised this way are more pleasant to be around.

A trap for parents is that they sometimes seek to apply a formula approach to family life. If mom and dad have a particular affinity for certain practices (or disdain for others), their preferences can become family law. The problem arises when one of their children doesn't embrace their particular approach. It is the wise parent who examines such situations and takes care *not* to overstep one's boundaries in parenting.

Some examples:

- Some families consider that young ladies should always wear dresses or skirts. There is nothing immoral about such a requirement. However, what if, as a girl grows up, she wants to make other clothing choices? Providing she has been instructed in modesty and appropriate dress from a Scriptural perspective, is she sinning if she wishes to dress otherwise?
- There are families who spend time outlining a five year, ten year, or hundred year plan for themselves and future generations. Is it appropriate for parents to tell young children what they will be doing well into their adult years? I wonder how many would have wanted to be compelled to follow such plans of their own parents. If we view our offspring as property, we will mandate such things. If we view them as those entrusted to our care, we will seek to influence and persuade.

There are many other areas that could be cited. My point is that, as children grow, we move from actively directing their lives to helping them take more and more responsibility, teaching them to exercise Biblical self-government in the process. Their choices may be in line with the faith without being carbon copies of ours. Especially for those of us who came to faith as adults, we need to recognize that our children are being raised in a different context than we had, and we should exercise care *not* to come across that we own their consciences, their lives, and their futures.

Ownership of our children belongs to God alone. We would do well to examine our thinking and actions regularly, to be certain that we do not overstep our jurisdiction as we endeavor to be obedient to God's Word in our role as parents—a most terrifying and joyful calling, indeed.

22

When Our Heroes Disappoint Us

Social media lights up when a well-known and well-loved celebrity dies in a deliberate suicide or an accidental one by drug overdose. On purpose or unintended, the person is still dead and fans are heart-broken. More questions abound than answers. After all, don't fame, wealth, and preferential treatment bring about happiness?

The words *hypocrisy* and *acting* have similar meanings in the Greek. A good actor can convince you of words, ideas, and motives that he doesn't hold. Whether he makes you laugh or cry, he is pretending. What's more, with the state of technology today, actors go to work on a set, and much of the actual context in which they are placed is a bare propless studio, with a background inserted during the editing process. So, these "hypocrites" *really* are playing dress-up and pretend. Yet, their adoring fans credit them with super heroic powers, clever comebacks, breathtak-ing stunts, and beautiful complexions to boot. How difficult it must be to have to be "regular" when the silver screen has made you bigger than life, and when the "you" loved by the fans is not the real you at all!

There is a lesson for all of us, parents especially, in times such as these. Have we made ourselves "bigger than life" to our children? Have we pretended that we know all the answers? Do we cover up mistakes and bad judgments so that we don't lose our "superhero" status in their lives? Do we cover up abusive situations in our families and churches to escape the shame of the truth being found out? Are we well-versed in being "hypocritical actors"?

I remember the first time each of my children learned that I didn't know everything. It usually happened within the context of an event we were experiencing together for the first time. Inevitably, I would get a "Why did that person do that?" question. When I responded that I didn't know, their looks were incredulous: "What do you mean you don't know?"

These responses were rendered in frustration and annoyance. After all, they wanted answers, and they wanted them immediately. Somehow or another, I had tarnished their view of me. Keep in mind that I never claimed to know all things. In fact, in my eyes, I had spent a good deal of time teaching them that only God knew all things. But, obviously, the message hadn't been delivered clearly enough.

We need to make sure we don't convey (advertently or inadvertently) that we have all the answers, and that problematic situations need to be covered up. And, we need to make sure that we don't place that burden on others. I cannot help but think that celebrity suicides, often the end of the line for depression, addiction, and broken relationships, occur when celebrities are weary of keeping up their upbeat public persona in the midst of excruciating inner-personal lives. After all, their fan-base demands that they hide their vulnerabilities and masquerade their hurt (either inflicted upon or received from others). They are caught in the trap of having an image to uphold in order to continue to reap financial benefits and fame.

It's time we evaluate, in ourselves and our families, how much we have appropriated from the fantasy world of the celebrity, and make sure that we don't mimic the pretense of well-adjustment in our own lives when, in fact, we are desperately hurting.

The Scripture tells us to bear one another's burdens. Keep in mind that this instruction also means we need to share our burdens. After all, if someone won't share, another cannot bear. We must learn to recognize when others are expecting too much of us, and when we are doing the same with them. In the process, we'll find that the hurt, horror, or shame that can lead someone to take his/her own life, is much more easily confronted when we take off the masks of pretense. We may fool others, but we've not fooled God.

23

The Three Rs of Building the Kingdom

Nothing is quite so distressing as witnessing brothers and sisters in the faith at odds with one another. Even those who are not part of the disagreement can get pulled into the conflict because the parties in disagreement want mutual friends and acquaintances to side with them. I can tell you I have been on all sides of such turmoil and there is no enviable position in the lot.

Social media tends to aggravate such conflicts because "liking" the post of another seems to indicate that you are in full agreement with every aspect of that person's life and views. Likewise, it is so easy to click the "post" button before you have had a chance to measure your words and possibly "sleep on" your response. For something called *Facebook*, people tend to hurt each other without confronting each other face-to-face.

None of us who are still on this earth are fully sanctified, and that reality needs to be taken into consideration. Also, because social media doesn't lend itself to evaluating body language, mole hills can turn into mountains almost instantaneously. Furthermore, it is all too easy to fail to recognize that in their service to God, some of our brothers and sisters have a different focus than we do. Because their area of concern or priority sometimes steps on our toes, doesn't mean they are our enemies. We would do well to recognize the three Rs of fulfilling the Great Commission:

Repair—Some are called to help the broken, distraught, and abused. By the very nature of the function they perform, there will be those who distrust their motives and disagree with their priorities, especially if they call attention to areas of systemic, problematic practices.

Restore—Some are called to assist those who have violated God's covenant, have repented, and want to be restored into fellowship. Again, by nature of the focus of this kind of ministerial effort, there will be those who make assumptions about the motives involved and take issue with their loyalty to God's Word.

Reconstruct—Some are called to rebuild the culture from the bottom up, focusing their attention on education, family, and establishing a firm foundation for the future. Because this is such a comprehensive undertaking, many of these people can be very outspoken. Some assign the labels of "judgmental," "arrogant," and "unloving" to these efforts, claiming that those who advocate in these areas are not compassionate and come across in a non-Christ-like fashion.

If you cannot relate to these scenarios, count yourself blessed. But I have witnessed (and am witnessing) situations like these all around me. As flawed individuals working out our salvation with fear and trembling, we are bound to irritate, confound, enrage, and/or wound those within the family of God. I don't say this to commend these occurrences, but to point out that they are inevitable. Without God's law, we wouldn't have a prayer to resolve our difficulties with each other, and that is why it needs to be the bedrock of how we operate. We would also do well to acknowledge that we don't always have all the pertinent information at hand, and should be cautious about relying on our first impressions. Instead, we must consult the Word of God to come to proper conclusions.

It is good to remember that there were conflicts among those in the early church and there were times when good people found it difficult to work side by side. It's too easy from where we sit to assume that serious issues did not arise among the Biblical saints we look to as examples.

I believe we need to acknowledge these three Rs and remember a fourth one: We are all *relatives* if we are united to Christ, and our enemies should only be classified as enemies if they are truly the enemies of God.

24

Guiding the Conversation

Many times women I speak with lament that they don't have opportunities to share their faith. Those who stay at home with their children especially feel as though they have limited access to unbelievers. But the truth is quite different.

First, a woman's family is a great mission field. Even those born into a believing family need to be taught the Christian faith and discipled into a life that lives out God's law-word in practical ways. This should never be minimized as these sorts of interactions on a day-to-day basis will have a greater lasting value than occasional, infrequent exchanges with others.

That said, women have many chances to be salt and light to those outside their families. On any given day, a woman may have to deal with a service repair person, a customer service representative, a grocery clerk, parents at sporting activities, music teachers, store owners, and neighbors. The way to engage them into a mindset of Biblical thinking is to initiate topics and small talk that will guide the conversation into sharing a Biblical worldview.

Some suggestions:

Neighbor: "I notice that your children don't go to school. Do you do that homeschooling thing?"

Answer: "Yes we do. We made that choice because we want to educate our children in more than academics. As Christians, we want them to learn how to be responsible and competent in all areas of life. By the way, if you ever need anything during the day, we're home so we'd be happy to help you. God bless you."

Grocery clerk: "Are all those children yours? I mean, it looks like you are shopping for a sports team."

Answer: "Every single one of them is a blessing from God. We shop here because the prices are reasonable and the quality of food is good. I'm glad this store is close by. By the way, let me introduce you to my children (give names). Kids, say hello to (give name, and then make sure to say hello by name each time you frequent that store)."

Service repairman: "This washing machine looks like it gets a lot of use."

Answer: "Yes, with this many children we use it a lot. Do you mind if my older children watch as you fix it? We are a homeschooling family, and I'm eager for them to learn things I'm not able to teach them. Someday if God blesses them with families, it will be a great benefit if they have some idea as to how to fix things."

Of course, you'll need to adapt the exchanges that fit into the circumstance and your particular situation. But you can always be salt and light, even in the most mundane of interactions. Give it a try. I bet you will be surprised at the results.

25

Until the Nets are Full

The apostle Peter certainly ranks as one of the most colorful persons portrayed in Scripture. Here was a married, hard-working man who was full of passion, impetuosity, and love for the Lord. Yet, like us, he was a flawed man, governed at times by fear, pride, and anxiety. How fitting that the Lord of lords would choose this man to be among those who would lead a small band of disciples to change the world.

In Luke 5, there is an account that has a profound lesson for all of us who claim the name *Christian*. Peter, having just had a fruitless night fishing with no catch at all, has Jesus in his boat preaching to an eager crowd. Now, I can tell you, having been married to a salesman for almost forty years, nothing quite discourages a man like the reality that despite his efforts, he has nothing to show for them. I imagine that just as a salesman evaluates himself according to the number of sales he's made in a day, a fisherman evaluates himself by the fish he catches.

After the preaching is done, Jesus instructs Peter to cast his net over the boat. Peter, "knowing" that while Jesus may be a great preacher, He doesn't know that much about fishing, tells Him that there is no point in doing so, because they went the entire night without catching any fish. But, Peter then does something radical —he obeys. And in his obedience, he catches so many fish that his nets begin to break. Jesus then tells Peter that there will be a greater catch of men than the fish in the boat.

Many of us become discouraged when we share our faith with loved ones, friends, and neighbors who many times could not care less about what we are saying. We get tired of hearing our own voices and the likely response that we are being judgmental, legalistic, or religious fanatics. But, just as Peter obeyed when Jesus told him to cast his net once again, we must be ready, willing, and eager to persevere in the Kingdom activity we've been called to.

Looking back over the years that I have been actively endeavoring to obey the Great Commission, it has been discouraging at times. Matters that were so plain to me seemed to fall on deaf ears. However, today, by God's grace, I am privileged to experience nets that seem to be overflowing. What is the difference? God's timing is the simple answer. My job has never been to determine the "catch," but to faithfully cast my net.

All of us are given a window of time to serve the Lord here on earth. When we get weary, wondering where the finish line will be, it is good to adopt this perspective: *Until the nets are full!*

General Index

Note: the letter *n* in a page reference indicates that the subject is referenced in a footnote on that page; e.g., "dowry, 60n9" refers to footnote 9 on page 60.

also church, impotency against perversion

anxiety, 1, 137. *see also* fear

Arnold, Benedict, 60

authority
absolutizing the relative, 28–30
Biblical hierarchy, 13, 19
delegation vs. covenantalism, 15, 16, 17
men submitting to God, 18, 27–28, 85
conditional submission, 24–25, 26, 28–29, 36–37, 84
cooperating with, 9
divine right authority, 28–29
of fathers (*see* fathers)
of husbands (*see* husbands, authority of; submission)
improper use of, 4, 11, 19
vs. lording over, 27
proper use of, 4, 19
servant rulership, 19
spiritual, 2
usurpation of, 12–13, 15

automation, 116

autonomy, 25, 40, 70, 116, 117

B

babysitting. *see* children, outsourcing childcare

baptized paganism and secularism. *see* syncretism

battle of the sexes, 39

bearing burdens, 69, 132

beauty, 27, 43n3, 87

Bethual, 41

Bible. *see* law-word of God

birthday, 126

bitterness, 19

Blackstone, William
Commentaries on the Laws of England, 122

blasphemy, 117

blessings, 7, 35–36, 40, 112n2

body parts. *see* teaching, children, about their bodies

bridegroom, defined, 43–44

burden bearing, 69, 132

business, 13, 17, 28–29, 116, 137
entrepreneurship, 87–88

C

calling. *see also* vocations
distinctions in marriage, 25
helping children find theirs, 5–6, 103–104, 103n8, 129–130
preparation and education, 7, 9, 103–104, 103n8 (*see also* education)
understanding one's calling, 4

campaign management, 96

capital punishment. *see* death penalty

CAPTCHA, 26n3

careers. *see* callings; vocations

catechism, 55

celebrities, 8, 131–132

Chalcedon Foundation, 79, 126

charity, 78, 88

chaste conversation coupled with fear, 39

chastity. *see* purity and chastity

children. *see also* motherhood
comprehension of truth, 55
with disabilities, 110–111
disciplining, 55, 90, 91, 129

finding a good wife, 14, 43, 82
joining of two families, 48
parents' role, 43
pre-marital counseling, 29
prenuptial agreements, 44n6
teaching young children, 74
wifehood, 86
unity in, 22, 23, 28, 39
vows of, 29
wives (*see* wifehood)
Martha and Mary. *see* Mary and
Martha
martial arts, 63
Mary and Martha, 1
Matthew, 117
Matthew 18 protocol, 61–62
maturity, revolting against, 89
meaning and meaninglessness, 71,
99, 100
meat and milk. *see* milk and meat
of the Word
media, 48, 56, 107, 109–111, 112–119,
115, 123. *see also* social media
medicine. *see* health and nutrition
men
abdicating responsibility, 3
absence of, 3
abusing authority, 3, 11, 12
headship, 12
learning from women, 1, 9, 82, 83
menstruation, 26
mentorship of younger women. *see*
Titus 2 women
metaphysics, 116, 117
milk and meat of the Word, 27, 31, 38
ministry
day-to-day, 135–136
to the hurting, 133 (*see also* abuse;
victims)
library, 122

Reconstruction (*see*
Reconstruction)
to the repentant, 134
vocational, 7 (*see also* vocations)
misogyny (so-called) in Scripture,
49. *see also* feminism
misprision, 78. *see also* abuse,
protecting abusers
missions, 19
modesty, 65–66, 74, 115, 129
Moffatt, James, 26
money, 97
motherhood, 79–92
adequacy to teach, 105–106
being a good example, 91
childbearing, 42, 87, 128
as highest expression of
womanhood, 9
learning from children, 107–108
multi-tasking, 87
nursing, 87
pregnancy, 42, 87
Mother Nature, 121
movie ratings, 115. *see also* media
murder, 64, 71, 117
music, 103, 135

N

Nabal, 13–14
neutrality, the myth of, 120, 121
New Covenant theology, 71
New Deal, 8
New Testament
overriding God's Law, 53
new world order, 48
Noah, 117
noetic effects of sin, 120, 121
nutrition. *see* health and nutrition

mutual submission, 32
not to be enforced by husbands, 24
vs. subservience, 9
teaching younger women to
submit, 3
trump card, 23–24
suffering in silence. *see under* abuse
suicide, 54, 110, 131–132
superheroes, 117
syncretism, 7–8, 110

T

teaching
children (*see also* education;
homeschooling)
about sex, 57, 73
about their bodies, 74
about the "real world," 56–57,
62, 73
stranger danger, 74
the Bible, 55–56, 86, 91, 114, 117
fundamentals of, 55, 86, 91
helping children find their
calling, 5–6, 103–104,
129–130
manners, 136
practical examples, 6, 73, 107,
136
to respond to sexual abuse,
58–59, 68, 74–77 (*see also*
abuse)
responsibility, 5, 88, 90, 94
self-government, 129–130
worldview, 56, 86, 91, 98, 100,
114, 128–129
goal of, (*see* men)
qualifications for, (*see* men)
respect for personal space, 74

younger men, 28
younger women, 3, 28, 79, 84, 89,
90 (*see also* Titus 2 women)
to prepare for marriage (*see*
marriage, preparing for)
Ten Commandments, 55, 64. *see
also* law-word of God
textbooks, 100. *see also*
homeschooling, materials and
curriculum
text, defined, 112–113
theft, 64, 117
"The Luxury of Words" (poem), 108
theology. *see also* reading
excluding women from, 1–2, 9, 83
importance of Biblical literacy,
18, 31, 68, 75n7, 84, 99–100,
102, 103, 113
as overwhelming to women, 83, 98
Thomism, 8
thought life, 112–119
time management, 93–94
tithes, 18, 22, 78
Titus 2 women, 3–4, 28, 79–80,
83–84, 89–91, 90–91, 95
tokens of virginity, 45–46, 47
tongue. *see* speech
training children. *see* children,
training in fear and
admonition of God
treason, 60
trump card. *see under* submission
trusting God, 89, 92
false versions of, 36, 50–51

U

United States of America, 28–29
unity in Christ, 9, 134

Scripture Index

CPSIA information can be obtained
at www.ICGtesting.com
Printed in the USA
FSOW02n0540300816
24337FS